Selecting The Brass Ring

How to hire really happy, really smart people (and pay them really well)

(the complete work)

by Rex W. Castle

Copyright © 2016 by Rex Castle
All rights reserved
For information about permission to reproduce selections, which by the way should be no problem, from this book, email rcastle263@gmail.com.

This work is dedicated to my wife, Danette
and daughter, Erin,
who provide me an exceptional understanding of
what "really happy" really looks like

Contents

Why Use this Book/Journal vi

Chapter 1 Why Choose This Merry-Go-Round 1

Chapter 2 Grasping The Ring 13

Chapter 3 Missing The Ring Badly 29

Chapter 4 Grabbing The Ring 53

Chapter 5 Stopping the Merry-Go-Round 79

Chapter 6 Selecting The Ring 119
    Relationship Building Skills 137
    Customer Service Skills 148
    People Skills (the ability to love people) 160
    Communication Skills 167
    Problem Solving Skills 172
    Ability to Follow Rules and/or Procedures 177
    Other Attributes 182

Chapter 7 After the Merry-Go-Round Stops 189
    A Note Regarding Pay 190
    On Interviewing and Taking Notes 207
    The Next Most Difficult Question 212

Ensuring Your Selection of The Brass Ring (or Contact Me) 237

Appendix Your Table of Contents Journaling Adventure 241

Why Use this Book/Journal

I wrote this book over a decade ago. I sent it to multiple publishers and received really nice rejection letters. Most read something like "we really like the writing style, but it's not really a topic we cover."

On a few of course I heard crickets.

People are just really busy.

I next wrote a parable of the following and I didn't even bother with publishing houses, but self-published through amazon.com, which is a monumentally easy process. I haven't moved into publishing through them on the Kindle, but if it's as easy as publishing through their self-publishing house, it has to be way, way easy. I opted to publish this book in this way as well.

The book you hold is special for a number of reasons...well, beyond the writing.

First, you'll notice on almost every page little numbers next to each line.

If you find something you think is worth remembering drop down to the bottom of the page. On the first block of 5 stars rate this line (paragraph) you think is worth remembering: say 1 star means "pretty good" and 5 stars means "I have to remember this." Then, on the line next to the stars, write the little number that appears next to the line you just read.

Make sense? You're able to evaluate what you've read as you've read and unlike a simple highlight when you come back you can immediately see how important you found the line.

You don't have to do this on every page, but only when you run across something you decide is critical.

Second, when I read I sometimes think of ideas. Some are related to what I'm reading. Some maybe reference something I read somewhere else. And some ideas I just sort of makeup.

The longer lines at the bottom of each page are for these thoughts, these notes.

Third, and this is really important. Too many of us have great ideas that sort of disappear over time.

They get stuck in a highlighted book on a bookshelf or noted in our Kindle or other electronic reader or maybe we just write them down somewhere.

Regardless, they are rarely to be seen again.

After you write an idea at the bottom of a page, Turn this book over, so now you're looking at the blank back cover as though it's the front of the book.

Open the back cover and where "my contents" is printed (last page of this book), start on the top line and make a quick note about your idea (i.e., "A thought on hiring") and beside this quick note write the page number in this book where you wrote the idea (and, if appropriate or desired, maybe write the little line number next to the line that generated the idea that you just wrote in this book).

Continue reading and when this happens again…and again…repeat the preceding and fill this book, this journal, with your great ideas.

When this book fills up, too, any bookstore sells blank books. The way you use these is simply number the odd pages and then start writing your notes.

Your "my contents" works exactly the same way in these blank books.

In this way, you can return to this journal (and/or a future journal) to your "my contents" and find a valuable note in a matter of seconds.

Think about this for a minute. You're creating a personal library of ideas, thoughts, referenced material that you have immediate access to. Your ideas are no longer lost in a highlighted book somewhere, stuck in a drawer along with countless other notes or sitting in electronic oblivion on your Kindle or in some notepad on that laptop upstairs, or was it the one at the office, or did I put that on my iPad?

You can find an idea, a valued note in minutes even if your journaling library grows, which it will, to several journals.

Every week or two, it is quite easy and very quick to go back and review your ideas and notes. The only problem with this is this process dramatically engages and activates your brain and you'll therefore...yes...potentially need additional journals.

This "journaling" is one of the most powerful tools this book provides you.

Unlike other journals, however, you never have to leave this book.

Chapter 1
Why Choose This
Merry-Go-Round

The Brass Ring is very apropos to a discussion of hiring. We're on a merry-go-round and each time we pass the Brass Ring we reach for it and sometimes we're luckier than others and we catch the brass ring and other times we catch what we think is the brass ring and it turns out to be lead and still other times we just sort of spin around in circles. Sound like hiring?

30+ years ago, too, my wife and I were talking about this whole "career" thing. I was a fledgling writer, having just graduated college with a degree in English and filled with the hopes and dreams of older youth (I was a non-traditional student). I'd received some nice accolades from most my professors and many were impressed with my ability to put words on a page and with the ideas I generated behind those words. So I was destined, or so it seemed, to write.

☆ ☆ ☆ ☆ ☆

These lines are provided for your notes, thoughts and any other quotes you want to include. Then, you use these in conjunction with the Appendix to keep a very accurate and very quickly reference-able journal of everything related to hiring. A super, super tool!

These stars allow you to "rate" a sentence or paragraph and the small line numbers next to that rated sentence or paragraph go on this line. When you return you can quickly determine what is important and how important that "what" is.

☆ ☆ ☆ ☆ ☆

Somewhere in this "plan" life stepped in and I found a job and then a life's work and I headed off into human resources where sure enough I was destined to write, but short of the American novel I was writing policies and procedures and annual reports and putting together documents that accompanied training I created.

My wife always wanted a book from these fingers. She'd even picked out a title, which was a tad presumptuous, not to mention optimistic, but I liked the title: The Brass Ring. I started and stopped, or completed and discarded, maybe ten next great American novels. None of them were that great, but they were great practice. What you hold is a culmination of some of that work, but it's not a great American novel either. I'm glad, though, I finally got to use her title.

Selecting The Brass Ring is a piece about hiring based off two decades of working within human resources and based off a ton of reading, careful thought and experimentation (lots and lots of experimentation). I've taken grabbing the brass ring away from luck and timing and brought it into an arena where I'm rather shockingly more comfortable, science. And hence the title "Selecting" has little to do with reaching out and snaring something passing by; "Selecting" is science.

My last hire was my best. The one before that was my second best. The one before that second best was my next best. The one... You probably get the idea. With each successive hire I've more or less improved with the person I've picked. Some of this is luck. Some of it is timing. Most of it is the science of my Model. The work you hold is my Model and how to go about building one and how to go about hiring to one.

The following quote comes from Quintessential Careers:

"The premise behind behavioral interviewing is that the most accurate predictor of future performance is past performance in similar situations. Behavioral interviewing, in fact, is said to be 55 percent predictive of future on-the-job behavior, while traditional interviewing is only 10 percent predictive."

Since when is 5 out of 10 a good enough process in business? Think of anything we do in any business. Fifty percent. I can't imagine when I worked for Coca-Cola producing every other can of soda with the correct formula. I can't imagine working in banking making the correct change every other time. And, will our customers be satisfied if we blow off their next need? I cannot think of one single viable business or one single significant process where one in two is plenty good

3

enough. Okay, hitting homeruns in baseball. If every other shot was a ball over the fence, that would be a great outcome.

But when we hire, what many of us have in our employee handbooks refer to as "our most valuable asset," the instrument that can dramatically impact our business (negatively or positively), when we make this critical decision "55 percent predictive" is good enough. Right? Granted, 55 percent is better than 10 percent, but it's not close to good enough.

My Model raises that percentage to 75 percent. And, if we couple the Model with the 55 percent behavioral interviewing effort, we can raise the Model percentage to 80, 90 and often 100 percent. All the preceding of course is dependent on the time we take and ensure we do this hiring thing right. Can you imagine hiring exceptional performers 90 percent or 100 percent of the time? Would our businesses look any different than they do today?

But I didn't wake up one morning and start hiring exceptional employees.

The best way to describe most my early hiring decisions is that they were something of a tragedy. I had a friend of mine, a boss who turned into a friend, tell me once "Rex, a hard drive crashing isn't a tragedy because no one dies." As occasionally happens the god of fate looked down on my friend a couple of weeks later and obliterated his hard drive.

He was right no one died, but I knew in conversations with him he sometimes wished he had.

Poor hiring is a similar tragedy. Oh, sure, we read or hear about the spectacular cases where someone hires one of the goofballs with a gun and when the smoke clears and the dust settles we have a tragedy in its truest definition, but even our worst hiring decisions don't usually result in actual death, but rather result in a small piece of our organization getting sick, atrophying or dying.

And there's limited magic that can be brought to this equation. You can use my twenty+ years of doing this stuff, but some of my worst hiring decisions came just a few years ago. That's really what got me going again in my quest for something beyond behavior-based interviewing because what I was doing, which was mainly behavior-based interviewing, just didn't seem to be working. I was producing copious notes through monumental hand cramps and hiring the wrong person about 50 percent of the time. So, I guess, according to the way behavior-based interviewing is supposed to work, I was doing the best I could and achieving the best results it had to offer.

I was producing every other can of Coca-Cola right and by golly that was just good enough.

Most of us, I imagine, make a bad hiring decision, shrug our shoulders, say "oh well" and go on. I perseverate on the decision. I mull it over. I analyze what I asked, how I asked and what I missed. I look at my notes and lay awake at night wondering "what could I do better next time?"

That's where I was getting hung up with behavioral interviewing.

I didn't know how to take more copious notes. After years of trying to keep up writing on legal pads and then trying to read my hieroglyphics, I set my interviews up on a computer and would type furiously as the interviewee would watch in amazement and more probably amusement.

At the end of the interview I'd go through, reread my notes, make typo and word choice corrections. At the end of the process I'd print all my notes, punch three holes in the pages and put them in the most detailed 3-ring binders anyone could have produced. I'd sit and reread and reread my copious notes and admire my 3-ring binder. My General Counsel practically wet herself over the effort. But at the end of the process I was no closer to the right hire than I had been when I started. I simply had a lot more notes to look at and a pretty binder.

So, I'd just sort of blow off my copious notes and go with my gut and hire right give-or-take 50% of the time.

And the preceding is not to say behavior-based interviewing does not work. It does, but it works to a point. It's still reliant on interviewees guessing what we're asking, making stuff up, their presentation and our interpretations.

Lots of folks don't want to read a great deal about this hiring stuff either, having "more important" things to do with their time, like "write up" the employee we hired who has the bad attitude, rehire the position of the recent hire who just yelled a string of profanities at us that would make a sailor blush and stormed out, respond to the unemployment or EEO (Equal Employment Opportunity) complaint or sit down yet again with our attorney to discuss the upcoming deposition in the wrongful termination complaint that some %@#&! filed.

☆ ☆ ☆ ☆ ☆
☆ ☆ ☆ ☆ ☆
☆ ☆ ☆ ☆ ☆
☆ ☆ ☆ ☆ ☆
☆ ☆ ☆ ☆ ☆
☆ ☆ ☆ ☆ ☆
☆ ☆ ☆ ☆ ☆
☆ ☆ ☆ ☆ ☆

I understand constraints on our time. Read the next couple of paragraphs and they'll give you the guts of the rest of this work. If you get what you need out of the next couple paragraphs, stop reading— wow!

Alan, a friend of mine, went to start a new bank after ours sold. And I don't really know how people start a new bank. Do they get a bunch of folks in a room and everyone puts all the money they have in a big pot and someone then decides "yep, we have enough to start lending," or what? I just don't know. But that's what Alan did.

He couldn't afford a boots on the ground human resources guru like me, so he did the next best thing and took me to lunch. My advice is always free and sometimes it's worth at least that much. During the course of lunch he asked me if I could give him my overarching "HR philosophy."

I didn't need to mull that question too long as I had come to a rather stunning conclusion about the time I hired my last disaster and said "hire really happy, really smart people and pay them really well."

And the "smart" part came from a friend I was sharing my philosophy with. He said "I'd add 'smart.'" He had an applicant who was really smart and thoroughly overqualified for his position and so he decided to pass on her. A week later he was at a conference talking with another friend about how difficult a time he was having hiring someone and about this "really smart, overly qualified master's graduate he'd passed on." His acquaintance told him, "That's good Ron because if you hire too many smart people your company just keeps growing and growing and growing and pretty soon you have so much money you don't know what to do with it."

My friend contemplated this through a sleepless night and picked up the phone as early as he dared the next day and hired the really smart, overqualified master's graduate and just like his acquaintance had told him, his company has grown exponentially and my friend has hired a couple of other really smart, really overqualified people. He pays them really well and makes sure they're happy WHEN HE HIRES THEM.

So, I added "smart" to my equation.

"Hire really happy, smart people and pay them really well," of course, is a gross oversimplification, but the rest of the book basically reinforces that sentence. The next paragraph is important because I try to convince you to read, and to keep this document, my book, as your reference when hiring.

Eight paragraphs preceding this one I cleverly, almost subliminally, outlined a few expected outcomes of poor hiring (performance counseling, rehiring unemployment, EEO, legal action), but these time-consuming, resource-draining and morale-diminishing activities are really only a part of the expense-side of the equation—the real reason to read the following is to insure your work is fun, or more fun.

We spend too much of our lives involved in creating a successful company; we need to at the very least be having some fun. The folks we hire and supervise are a big part of creating that environment. And, like some women I've heard about, who have married men thinking they were going to "change" the man, have figured out, you can't change a grump into a happy camper because you shower him with affection, good humor and ice cream. Grumps are grumps. That's who they are and who they bring to work.

So, if you have the time, patience and inclination, take a whirl with me on a journey. At the end I will guarantee if you follow this strategy, you will hire the most amazing people on the planet and your company's profits will skyrocket like never before. I'm not sure what that guarantee is worth, but when I'm on Oprah and talking about my strategy and you've tried it and for some bizarre reason it didn't work for you, you can slam down your copy of the thing you're reading and

☆ ☆ ☆ ☆ ☆ _____
☆ ☆ ☆ ☆ ☆ _____
☆ ☆ ☆ ☆ ☆ _____
☆ ☆ ☆ ☆ ☆ _____
☆ ☆ ☆ ☆ ☆ _____
☆ ☆ ☆ ☆ ☆ _____
☆ ☆ ☆ ☆ ☆ _____

swear at the T.V. and then angrily shut it off or turn the channel—that's my guarantee. Or, you can also contact me because this process does work and it does work absolutely, so you may be doing something wrong as I failed in my explanation.

_____   ☆☆☆☆☆ _____
_____   ☆☆☆☆☆ _____
_____   ☆☆☆☆☆ _____
_____   ☆☆☆☆☆ _____
_____   ☆☆☆☆☆ _____
_____   ☆☆☆☆☆ _____
_____   ☆☆☆☆☆ _____
_____   ☆☆☆☆☆ _____

Chapter 2
Grasping for
The Ring

No one has time to hire. Posting the job, reviewing applications, conducting interviews, maybe conducting another round of interviews, extending an offer, training, etc., etc., etc. Following "the rules." No one has this kind of time.

As long as I've been doing this I've harped to managers that if we make a bad choice, the time on the frontend isn't nearly what will be required on the backend and that argument has rarely worked, even, surprisingly, with managers who have been on the backend.

I have a whole gaggle of examples I dredge up during any training I've done and regardless of how the story ends, how much it costs and how many buildings and careers are burned down in the process, I have always fought the battle of "I don't have the time." And more often than not they add "for this junk" as in "I don't have the time for this junk."

Sometimes, too, they'll just ask me to "hire someone," often adding "darn it" to the end of that statement.

Well, "you can pay me now, or…" You've taken a great step in exploring this alternative I refer to as my Model.

Successful selection often means not choosing the most qualified candidate. Wow! Let me illustrate as the "most qualified" turns out not to be the best candidate.

Work is many times a lot more than whether someone can do the job. There are a multitude of often dynamic and complex relationships that tend to get overlooked by the task list, the job description. Think about your top performers for a minute. What are his or her attributes you covet?

"Attitude" is always high on the list, "self-motivated," "fun" maybe, "smart" probably, "team player" almost always and the list goes on. Value grows when on your list comes an element also on the job description you're hiring from.

Even some position, which may be viewed as seemingly innocuous like a custodian or receptionist, has consequences of relationships.

When I was being considered for the Human Resources Information Specialist position at Coke I was called in for a second interview. "Rex, my future boss began, I've run into something that I'm not sure how to deal with and so I thought I'd just ask you."

"Okay," I said and wondered "what the heck?"

☆☆☆☆☆ _____
☆☆☆☆☆ _____
☆☆☆☆☆ _____
☆☆☆☆☆ _____
☆☆☆☆☆ _____
☆☆☆☆☆ _____
☆☆☆☆☆ _____

"Everyone I talk to says you're a great guy, easy to get along with, good sense of humor, very creative…" (I could go on listing my exceptional attributes probably for at least a couple three paragraphs, but the point is he was loading the question before the inevitable "but").

"…but some are concerned that you allow people to push you around and you're too helpful and don't know how to say no and that worries me."

"Mark," I began "I know where that comment is coming from. Right now I work in a group that is pretty tied into their titles and job responsibilities. We have Eric who is the programmer and Madge who is Eric's boss and oversees the technical side of the project and they both have their defined roles. We have Lonnie who is the project director and he has his defined role. And we have Carol the receptionist and folks don't really hang around Carol too much because 'she's the receptionist.'

I tend to help Carol. Like for instance she'd never used mail merge in Word before and so I typed and set up the letter and typed in a few addresses in the list file and showed her how all that stuff works. She, at that moment, thought I was pretty spectacular."

Mark was sitting and listening and I could tell he was wondering where this was leading.

"I do this for a number of reasons. First, if I have the time to help and something is technically 'not my job' what do I care? I have the time, I can move the organization forward because I have knowledge that will increase efficiency and nothing I'm doing suffers, so what's the downside? That people think I'm too helpful and get pushed around?"

But I knew Mark knew my preceding response was the standard "This organization is bigger than me and I'm just here to make it more successful" schlock that all interviewers hear and most see right through, so I continued, not to impress, but because the continuation was a more accurate definition of my thought process.

"Second, I help Carol for a purpose. She's the gatekeeper for our expense reports. When I turn in an expense report I usually have a check back that afternoon or the following morning.

One of my coworkers actually waited three weeks to get her check back because she didn't sign the expense report and Carol forwarded it anyway and it had to come back and it sat on Carol's desk and then she forwarded it to its originator and not by walking across the foyer and handing it to my coworker, or picking up the phone and telling her, or simply blurting something out the door, but through interoffice mail and that meant going back over to main campus and getting sorted and getting resent back to who else? Carol, the same Carol who had sent it.

Then it sat in Carol's in-box for a day or so and she finally put it in my coworker's mail slot where it sat for who knows how long, since most mail Carol simply hand delivered and so none of us ever thought about checking our mail slot.

Carol, when she told me the story, thought that the preceding was pretty gosh darned funny. What was interesting, too, is the coworker

☆ ☆ ☆ ☆ ☆ _____
☆ ☆ ☆ ☆ ☆ _____
☆ ☆ ☆ ☆ ☆ _____
☆ ☆ ☆ ☆ ☆ _____
☆ ☆ ☆ ☆ ☆ _____
☆ ☆ ☆ ☆ ☆ _____
☆ ☆ ☆ ☆ ☆ _____

whose check was delayed thought Carol was the biggest idiot that ever wandered the planet. 'Why didn't she simply call me?' she whined."

"She wasn't being idiotic. Carol was insuring she wasn't going to be pushed around and treated with disrespect."

Recognition began to come to Mark's face at this point as he smiled and began nodding his head.

"So I'm currently in a position where I need to get things done through others, but I haven't the authority to simply ask someone to do it and expect they're going to jump up and down because I'm asking. I get things done because I do things for others and we scratch one another's backs. Maybe that makes me 'too helpful' and a 'pushover,' but I think it makes me smart."

He hired me, so I guess he agreed. That wasn't the story I wanted to share with you, but it is a story that illustrates the seemingly innocuous positions, or probably a better way to say it would be the positions that a lot of folks do not recognize for their importance, in an organization are positions that are gatekeepers in nature or, as is the case of the custodian, may be a position that assists with safety, convenience or comfort. They're integrally tied to others in the organization and each helps move the organization forward...or not.

I had a custodian tell me that he ordered the roughest, meanest, nastiest toilet paper he possibly could find for our CEO's bathroom because the CEO was "such a jerk and his bathroom deserved the crustiest toilet paper 'I' can find."

☆☆☆☆☆
☆☆☆☆☆
☆☆☆☆☆
☆☆☆☆☆
☆☆☆☆☆
☆☆☆☆☆
☆☆☆☆☆
☆☆☆☆☆

The incredible part of this story is that the custodian admitted to "sampling" toilet papers until he found the most excruciatingly painful one and he even solicited vendors' assistance and they were happy to help him figure out how to "get the jerk" because they'd had bosses like that as well. And when the CEO complained, the custodian went through the process again and replaced the excruciatingly painful toilet paper with an equally as excruciating substitute until the CEO quit complaining.

I had an administrative assistant tell me once that he took great delight in killing every plant his general manager's wife brought into the building (and she brought in a lot). The creative measures he took to kill plants, too, were simply inspiring (in that sort of horror movie type inspiration).

He urinated one plant to death.

I had two friends who were garbage men. They worked as a team. The trucks they worked on were not hydraulic and they'd have to pick up the trash cans and empty them by hand. Their boss was one of those kick in the seat managers who never had a kind word to say about anything or anyone, but here was the clever part, whenever anyone was out sick, absent or hurt, the manager had to fill in. In turn each of my friends would try to out lift the other and pile more and more trash on top of the original trash can at their next stop. The object was not to be macho; the object was to injure themselves and go home "and let that _____ do it."

☆ ☆ ☆ ☆ ☆ _____
☆ ☆ ☆ ☆ ☆ _____
☆ ☆ ☆ ☆ ☆ _____
☆ ☆ ☆ ☆ ☆ _____
☆ ☆ ☆ ☆ ☆ _____
☆ ☆ ☆ ☆ ☆ _____
☆ ☆ ☆ ☆ ☆ _____

The point is these people are critically important to the functioning of a company and when we slight them we do so at our own peril and to the detriment of the company.

Jobs are like that. One position is connected to the next through a relationship and so as we get deeper into this whole idea of selection keep in mind one of my suggestions for selection and that is to be cognizant of the relationships this position touches because the relationships are critical to the success not only of the position for which you are hiring, but for every position the person you hire will come in contact with. A couple of examples might help solidify this point.

I made a phenomenally poor personnel decision a few years ago. My payroll/benefits person, Adrianne, decided to go off to a new career (really, a completely different direction). I was happy for her, but my life went from bliss to misery in the six weeks or so before she finally couldn't come back and help Darlene, who I left drowning in the ocean of work Adrianne managed to take care of.

I had attempted to put the two positions, Payroll and Benefits, together and unless you have someone truly phenomenal to attempt this feat, and your company is relatively small and very evolved technology-wise, the sky will cave in and everyone will want to kill you in pretty short order.

So, with Darlene drowning, but semi-okay at payroll, I made the decision to hire a benefits person. We, I at least had a cohort in the decision, did interviews, found someone who seemed "okay" and hired

Mike. Mike came in and from day one was a drag on morale. Nothing made him happy except when everyone seemed miserable and then Mike was about the happiest guy on planet earth. This went on for just a few weeks and then Mike left, filed unemployment and claimed "hostile work environment."

After the unemployment hearing the hearing officer wrote in his response "I've seen hostile work environments and on a scale of 1 to 100, where 100 is the worst, this one is about a 5 or 6." The point of this story is not to point to Mike and say "what an idiot," although I could easily support that argument. The point of this story is to say when we hire the wrong person our other good employees suffer and we expend a ton of energy in areas probably best described as counter-productive. Of course, this is the exact opposite of what we want to happen.

Previously, I had two other people handling Payroll and Benefits. Esther was a benefits guru. She was so good I could put up with her rather odd personality (she would complain because her coworkers sometimes disturbed her work by discussing the weekend football game on Monday mornings). Ell was my payroll person and she did a fair job. I had been steadily working with her to bring her up to at least "okay."

One day I returned from lunch and one of the other folks who shared our office area said "Man, Rex, your folks went after each other a bit ago. It was a real 'cat fight.'"

Long and short was that Esther and Ell had been in a screaming match in front of the other employees. When Esther came back from lunch she came to my office and we talked about what had happened. She was essentially tired of Ell's excuses and lack of competence. When Ell returned she came to my office although Esther had returned to her desk and Ell and I discussed what had happened. The facts were not really at issue. Most critical to me was we were human resources and there had been raised voices and a "cat fight." This was simply unacceptable.

I rarely have two employees sit together as I address personnel concerns, but in this case that is what I did. At the end of the day, I invited both to my office and I laid out the facts and I laid out my expectations. I told them both that the behavior was unacceptable and would not happen again and if it did I would fire "anyone who was involved regardless of who started it."

I next turned to Ell and said "And, Ell, I need you to understand something. Esther is my right and often my left hand. If she ever comes in here and says 'I'm leaving or Ell is leaving, but I'm not working with her any longer' then my next conversation will be with you and you'll leave. I would take this opportunity to learn from Esther as she's a lot better at what she does than you are at what you do and you can learn a great, great deal from her. Any questions?"

Esther had indeed put up with Ell's behavior, attitude and lack of competence for long enough. I had been remiss in my responsibility as a supervisor. My intent was to correct this part of the problem that day.

☆ ☆ ☆ ☆ ☆
☆ ☆ ☆ ☆ ☆
☆ ☆ ☆ ☆ ☆
☆ ☆ ☆ ☆ ☆
☆ ☆ ☆ ☆ ☆
☆ ☆ ☆ ☆ ☆
☆ ☆ ☆ ☆ ☆
☆ ☆ ☆ ☆ ☆

Ell worked another couple of months and then left. It wasn't a great loss, but it was too bad. She was relatively young and could have learned a great deal from Esther had she been open to it, but she was not. I should have probably demanded more from her and insisted on a close working relationship, but I didn't. Whenever there's a personality conflict the manager is responsible for ending it. I don't care if folks want to play in the sandbox together after hours, but during work the sandbox and the rules are mine and they will play together or the best one stays. Honest conversation is the only way I know to approach such problems. But, again, this relationship put one of my best employees through a trial that she didn't need to be put through and I was irritated with myself for not addressing the situation more forcefully and sooner. I was irritated for having made the decision to hire a problem in the first place.

The preceding taught me, or reinforced in me, the value of building a work group composed of sustaining relationships. This gets very difficult as organizations expand, but within a workgroup building these relationships is essential to a manager's success. Therefore, "relationship" building, or rather "relationship connectivity" became something of an overarching selection principal in my world of work. It is one of my foundational principles in making a hiring decision. I find it stands alone in terms of importance when compared to almost anything else I've ever dreamed up. Relationship connectivity—know it, think about it, understand it, hire for it.

Unfortunately, when you have "principles" you sometimes have to exercise them even though the decision is one that occasionally haunts you for a bit. I was hiring for a human resources management position.

I had just lost a manager who was technically sound, but she was a relationship nightmare. In this position I needed someone who could build respectful relationships with employees, managers, me and my boss and her subordinate, the corporate general counsel. Ernie, our general counsel, was actually in a parallel position to mine. Dorothy was the chief counsel for the company and I had a dual reporting relationship between her and the general manager.

She was also older, having been the second woman to have graduated from her law school. She was a feminist and on the side liked to do pro-bono work with immigration law. She had also been around since the company came together and an employee advocate, but was also the company's primary advocate. These roles of course competed at various times during my tenure and helping to balance this often conflicting relationship was always of paramount concern to me.

Dorothy, too, was always an advocate for hiring females and I was very understanding of this fact as the human resources manager that had left, leaving me this open position had been female, and she and Dorothy were seemingly always on the same side and I was often on the other. At the same time Dorothy was supportive of my efforts to get this HR person to build stronger relationships. I desperately wanted to hire a female for this role, as my first decision, for my direct assistant, I ended up hiring a male who was heads above the competition, but I also hired to the chagrin of Dorothy.

"Male or female" is not of course a legal criteria for hiring anyone (outside of a midwife), but this was simply my, and many times our, reality. You don't "not hire" someone because she's female, but you keep searching for the next more qualified candidate (I've reread that last sentence like fourteen times and I know its structure is awful; let's agree it's awful and move on).

Easily, in my quest to hire the perfect Human Resources Manager, my most qualified applicant was a young, white male.

"Shoot."

I entered the interview with a sense of dread, but in sort of a positive way as I really did want a very qualified person, but I rarely had someone disqualify themselves during an interview and on paper this kid was a dynamo. Usually folks are on their best behavior during an interview and they sometimes, but not often, slip. Chuck would be a tough one, too, because he, like me, had a number of years of experience in human resources and so I knew I had someone who knew what they were doing in an interview.

And Chuck was probably my eighth or ninth interview. I thought for as long as I remember that behavior-based interviewing where you ask open-ended questions about specific things someone has done in their past (rather than yes and no questions or speculative questions) was always the way to go. Behavior-based interviewing had made sense to me from the moment I was introduced to the concept early in my career. I also thought a behavior-based interview was by necessity long and my interviews generally ranged from 90 minutes to two hours and we often took a break at about the two-thirds point.

☆☆☆☆☆ _____ _____
☆☆☆☆☆ _____ _____
☆☆☆☆☆ _____ _____
☆☆☆☆☆ _____ _____
☆☆☆☆☆ _____ _____
☆☆☆☆☆ _____ _____
☆☆☆☆☆ _____ _____

Chuck was a breeze. Every time I'd ask a question he'd have an answer waiting. He'd done everything, seen everything, worked on everything imaginable. This was rather confounding as he seemed to be about sixteen-years-old, but he had been fortunate. Fresh out of college he'd gotten in on the ground floor of a company that just started growing and growing and growing and finally stopped recently with a sale and he was looking for work, but gosh did he ever have the background.

We were manufacturing. They were manufacturing. We were distribution. They were distribution. We were consumables. They were consumables. I liked him from the moment he walked in the door and we seemed to hit it off without a lot of effort. That nagging question of "what about Dorothy the General Counsel, your boss, the feminist" kept coming up in my mind, but I was already working on my sales job including sending Chuck to meet Dorothy and interview with her. And, even with Dorothy wanting/ demanding females, my desire was to hire the most qualified regardless.

I had asked the full spectrum of questions and Chuck had put my mind at ease with every answer. He and I were laughing and carrying on as though we knew each other. That's really the great benefit to holding long and involved interviews—the candidate more often than not thinks you're his or her friend (in my experience less for females than for males). As the interview drew toward its conclusion I asked my new buddy the following question:

"Tell me about a time you were involved in some difficult litigation and what made this difficult and what the outcome was."

There was a long pause.

"I have to tell you, Rex, the worst litigation I was ever involved in was litigation I was never involved in."

I kind of laughed. "Okay, I'll bite. What does that mean?"

"Well, we had this guy who we terminated and he came around and filed a wrongful termination action on us claiming we terminated him because of his race and I really wanted to fight the deal because it was a crock, but I had this bimbo chick attorney..."

I don't recall what else Chuck said after that. I thought he had misspoke, but then he kept going and just as my brain was beginning to reengage he said it again. "Bimbo chick." After the interview I turned to Lee, who was my assistant and had sat through all the interviews with me, and taken very copious notes and Lee said "did you hear him say 'bimbo chick attorney' because I wrote it down...twice?"

"When I heard him say it I thought of Dorothy and how fast she would rip his head off if he ever said that around her," I responded. "All I could see after that was this little, bloody stump sitting across the table from me and getting that image out of my mind wasn't possible. Dorothy would just rip his head off."

I still hesitated on the decision. He was just that good, but in the end I couldn't get his pitiful little bloody stump after Dorothy took his head off out of my mind. If this had been a less important relationship I might have been swayed enough to hire him and then put him under a microscope and watch him...closely, but Dorothy was a primary relationship not only for the position Chuck interviewed for, but for me. And, there's a certain level of disrespect I cannot forgive and "bimbo chick" probably at least breeches that boundary pretty severely.

I made my decision, discussed it with Dorothy, and she was delighted to have a female assuming the reins of this important position. The female I hired was significantly less qualified than Chuck and unbeknownst to me she worked in the same office as Chuck's girlfriend. When I called Susie to offer the job she immediately went and joyfully told her coworkers. Chuck's girlfriend called Chuck and probably within five minutes of calling Susie, Chuck was on my phone.

He launched into a tirade that I have to this day never seen from any other applicant. "By gosh, he'd been around Susie and she wasn't even close to him in terms of qualifications and most her coworkers thought she was an idiot and..." I was really surprised, not that he would be disappointed and call me, but that this screaming, profane (I left out that part in my description, but he used some choice words) tirade would be his response. He had masked his personality in the interview about as good as anyone I had ever considered.

His response to my not hiring him, however, easily confirmed my decision.

His response confirmed my decision and I felt that way even during our phone call where I didn't tell him why I hired someone else (I didn't want him to cover this behavior from others), but I also never raised my voice. I hung up the phone thinking "what a jerk" and "I guess we weren't friends after all."

I took an extra step that I rarely take. My next call was to the President of our local Chapter of Human Resource professionals and I told her that she might want to quietly inform the members that this guy was out there looking for work and they may want to look at him real, real hard before making a decision. I try to tell folks the following and some actually listen. You have to be careful with how you behave around human resource people because we don't live insulated from one another. It's that relationship thing.

Behavior-based interviewing was responsible for uncovering Chuck. For a long time after this decision I embraced the process, but then I made a few bad decisions and my "what's wrong" demon started dancing around in my head again and I started looking more closely at the whole process of hiring and what follows is what so slowly evolved from that process.

☆ ☆ ☆ ☆ ☆
☆ ☆ ☆ ☆ ☆
☆ ☆ ☆ ☆ ☆
☆ ☆ ☆ ☆ ☆
☆ ☆ ☆ ☆ ☆
☆ ☆ ☆ ☆ ☆
☆ ☆ ☆ ☆ ☆

Chapter 3
Missing The
Ring Badly

We're going to talk about a process for hiring that I believe is almost infallible, but let me sort of step us into it by reliving some of what brought me to where I am.

A lot of folks have made great hiring decisions and they use a method of luck, intuition and interview questions they've found to be very effective throughout their careers. I'm not faulting them, or saying what they are doing is bad.

I think if you find something that works in an aspect of your life, you should probably keep using it. Maybe you want to look at my process and add bits and pieces and maybe you want to say "oh, cool stories" and ignore everything I say, or maybe you're like me and things sort of quit working somewhere along the road and you're kind of exploring other options.

That's what I consider this whole "build a Model and hire to the Model process" I have: Another option.

Please note, as well, at the beginning of this adventure names, places, times, etc. have been changed throughout this book, but, except for these changes the stories are 100% accurate—oh, and I do tend to embellish, of course, my naturally heroic nature as do we all.

I received a phone call one day from our San Antonio warehouse (I was with Coca-Cola at the time).

"Rex," the manager began, "I have a problem."

"What is it Tom?"

"Well, we hired..."

I stop here for effect. Note the "hired" at the end of that sentence before the ellipses. Throughout this book on selection whenever you see "hire," "hires," "hired," "hiring," etc. please think "this is probably important." And, as an aside, generally, whenever you see "we" used in the negative context think "I" as in "I the manager" who is responsible "put the car in the ditch on this one." In this case that "I" doesn't mean me, but I've had my fair share of mammoth mess ups, so none of us are immune.

The object isn't to admit we're less than perfect; it's to fix the imperfection. Otherwise, we're just being sort of stupid.

"Well, we hired a guy a few months ago, maybe you remember."

I oversaw a territory of 180,000 square miles with perhaps three dozen locations and 1,100 employees. I didn't remember.

The manager continued, "Well, never mind that, but this morning they found a dead girl in the lot next to our warehouse."

"Did this guy kill her?" I asked.

There was an uncomfortable pause.

"I'm not sure. I don't think so, but here's the deal. This guy we hired has everyone freaking out because he said 'it's no big deal. I killed someone once about a dozen years ago.'"

The manager went on to explain that the new hire said he'd been convicted and given deferred adjudication (that's the court's way of saying "if you're good for this many years we'll erase this from your record"). I'd never heard of deferred adjudication for killing someone, but I thought "this is Texas, so where justice is concerned just about anything is plausible."

I hung up the phone and contacted one of our attorneys. Ernie was flabbergasted, irritated and quite certain that no one can kill another and receive deferred adjudication. He was flabbergasted that we had made such a hiring decision and let me know his flabbergasted-ness. He was irritated for the same reason and let me know his irritation. But mostly he was confident that the employee was lying to the rest of our staff and telling a tall tale.

☆☆☆☆☆
☆☆☆☆☆
☆☆☆☆☆
☆☆☆☆☆
☆☆☆☆☆
☆☆☆☆☆
☆☆☆☆☆
☆☆☆☆☆

"Call the courthouse in the county where this allegedly took place and ask them to pull the paper record," Ernie commanded.

I wanted to call the courthouse anyway because I wanted to find out where our criminal background check had broken down. We did the computer search thing on the internet, and it was somewhat in its infancy at the time, and therefore I had taken the somewhat unique step of having a private investigator go to the courthouse and check the individual's paper record. If "we" had missed something, our private investigator was responsible. I wanted to hang this responsibility for missing this crucial piece of the hiring puzzle on someone else's head.

I called the courthouse and the phone rang and rang and rang and rang. I hadn't started calling until almost five on a Friday afternoon and I thought perhaps they had closed early. The following week I called repeatedly and the phone rang and rang and rang and rang. I called Monday morning and afternoon. Tuesday at different times. Wednesday...you probably get the idea. I made perhaps fifteen calls to the courthouse and no one ever picked up.

Until finally, the following Monday, I was into the sixth or seventh ring and a couple from hanging up when someone picked up the phone and there was silence.

"Hello," I said eventually.

"Yes," a lady, who seemed to be elderly, responded.

☆ ☆ ☆ ☆ ☆
☆ ☆ ☆ ☆ ☆
☆ ☆ ☆ ☆ ☆
☆ ☆ ☆ ☆ ☆
☆ ☆ ☆ ☆ ☆
☆ ☆ ☆ ☆ ☆
☆ ☆ ☆ ☆ ☆

"Is this the Deacon County Courthouse?" I asked.

Silence.

"Hello," I said.

"Yes," the lady responded.

"Is this the Deacon County Courthouse?" I asked my voice a bit higher.

"Yes," the lady responded.

"I need to speak to someone about…"

The conversation dragged on as this lady was the only person in the Deacon County Courthouse and the only one I could talk with and pulling tidbits of information out was monumentally difficult.

Somewhere in the conversation I mentioned that we had run an extensive computer background check on this person and probably come to the courthouse and found nothing. She responded "it may not be in the computer system yet as we're a little behind. Hold on and I'll check the 'other' file."

I didn't know what the "other" file was and was a little nervous to ask about it and as it turned out didn't have to.

The phone clunked down on the desk and I was "placed" on hold. Thirty seconds turned to a minute, turned to five minutes, turned to ten minutes. I was fearful to hang up as it had taken me a week to get in touch with someone. I was also fearful that this lady may have died on her way to get the "other" file and I'd be waiting on hold through my retirement and own death. Sometime later that day, my ears were sweaty as I transferred the phone back and forth, she returned.

"I found it," she said.

"Oh, already," I responded sarcastically and didn't receive even the slightest hint of a response.

"What does it say?" I prodded.

"Yep, he received 10 years deferred adjudication for vehicular manslaughter. He purposefully ran over a neighbor who wouldn't quit selling drugs to his kids and his neighbors' kids. Looks like he warned this drug dealer a number of times, so it was probably okay."

"When was his conviction?" I asked.

Long pause. "Looks like 1988."

"1988?" I asked.

"Yes, 1988."

"But that was twelve years ago," I said incredulously.

"I said we were a little behind," she said somewhat emphatically and definitely indignantly. And there was a long silence as she sat on her end of the phone I know feeling justified in pointing this out to me and I sat on my end of the phone just sort of stunned. I finally thanked her for her time and ended the conversation.

I hung up the phone and called Ernie, our attorney, explained the delay in getting back with him and also explained the elderly lady and the fact that this court was "a little behind."

We ended the conversation laughing about this fact and knowing that when it came to small county Texas (and probably other states as well) and smaller town Texas we could run into just about anything. I hung up, too, with a slight degree of vindication.

I called the hiring manager wanting to share what I had found and my attorney's flabbergasted-ness and irritation with the manager. I really didn't get much of a chance to share the "irritation" part because I at least make feeble attempts to approach things differently. Rather than trying to get my digs in and show my superiority and my higher pay grade I've always tried to think that fixing the problem was a better approach.

I shared what I thought of as a "tottering old lady" with the manager and what I thought of as "the decrepit old courthouse" with "the more decrepit old technology" with the manager. We had a good laugh.

☆☆☆☆☆
☆☆☆☆☆
☆☆☆☆☆
☆☆☆☆☆
☆☆☆☆☆
☆☆☆☆☆
☆☆☆☆☆
☆☆☆☆☆

Then he asked me what we could do about the convicted manslaughter-er who was freaking everyone out.

"Not much," I said. "He hasn't done anything in violation of policy."

"What about falsifying an application?" the manager asked.

"Well, duh, sure," I said. "Pull his app."

"Just a sec," the manager said and with that the phone clunked down on the desk and I was "placed" on hold. An ominous beginning.

The manager pulled the application. There's a set of checkboxes on the application, one for "yes" and the other for "no," beside the following question: "Have you ever pled guilty to, been convicted of, received deferred adjudication for, ever thought about doing anything that might result in, a felony?" (Actually the part about "thought about doing anything" isn't true, but the question is written without a lot of wiggle room.) And then you have to explain your actions if you check the "yes" box.

The manager looked at the application.

His voice low he said "He checked the yes box."

"He did?" my voice was a little strained, a little higher, a little more accusatory in the vein of "What's wrong with you idiots?"

"Yep," the manager said.

"What was the explanation?" I asked.

"Received 10-years of deferred adjudication for killing drug dealer with my truck," the manager read.

"Guess that kind of does in the whole falsification of application thing, doesn't it?" and even to this day I can read the dripping sarcasm in what I asked. I wasn't trying that hard at that moment to not be accusatory and not use my superior pay grade to let this manager have it. Even so he kept talking with me, which in hindsight, I'm grateful for.

Obnoxious managers, as I was being in this moment, don't usually get useful information; they generally just get confirming information, which is super if they're right. I felt I was being a right obnoxious manager at the moment (I don't believe, however, there's actually a time we can ever be "right" and "obnoxious").

"Guess not," he said.

"Can I ask you the process you used for hiring him?"

Remarkably the manager kept talking to me.

"He was the only one left," the manager said.

"What?" I asked.

☆ ☆ ☆ ☆ ☆
☆ ☆ ☆ ☆ ☆
☆ ☆ ☆ ☆ ☆
☆ ☆ ☆ ☆ ☆
☆ ☆ ☆ ☆ ☆
☆ ☆ ☆ ☆ ☆
☆ ☆ ☆ ☆ ☆
☆ ☆ ☆ ☆ ☆

"We had five applicants. Our first choice called, and he looked like the most qualified, and he had taken another job. The second one never returned any of our phone calls. The third one turned out to be from Michigan just looking for some place warmer and he wanted a moving allowance. The fourth one came in and we talked but he didn't want the job. So that left us with Brian and we hired him. I'm sorry, but I don't even remember looking at his application."

After I got out of therapy...Actually I never went to therapy, but there are definitely things managers do that will drive any human resources person over the edge. Stories like the preceding are such occasions.

Essentially, we chose Brian because a qualified candidate had found something else to do and Brian answered his phone.

My first suggestion for selection, therefore, is this: Always look at the application. And if you have managers who think they can actually glean something from a resume, please either require them to get a completely filled out application or get new managers. It's simply that rudimentary to the process and that important.

Here's the difference. A resume is a picture an applicant paints of himself or herself; an application is a picture where we have some limited control over what it is the applicant is painting.

And this is not to say that we wouldn't have hired this person even if we had looked at his application, after all he was the last one left standing in this rather vacuous applicant pool, but it is to say we would have known what we were hiring. And convicted felons, who have

☆ ☆ ☆ ☆ ☆ _____
☆ ☆ ☆ ☆ ☆ _____
☆ ☆ ☆ ☆ ☆ _____
☆ ☆ ☆ ☆ ☆ _____
☆ ☆ ☆ ☆ ☆ _____
☆ ☆ ☆ ☆ ☆ _____
☆ ☆ ☆ ☆ ☆ _____

served their time, are not necessarily, of course, excluded from employment, but we would have known what we were hiring.

And now as Paul might say "The Rest of the Story."

I put Brian on my radar screen. I thought the time would come where we'd probably be dealing with him on other issues. I had already received some grumbling comments from managers almost from the date of hire, so I was thinking with the dead body and everyone freaking out on me, this deal would only be a matter of time. I wasn't disappointed, or, more exact, I wasn't more disappointed as I didn't have to wait long.

Brian also had personal hygiene issues. He farmed pigs on the side and refused to bathe before coming to work, but after doing whatever it is pig farmers do with their pigs. As a mechanic he was frequently in a confined space and frequently in that space with others. Working in a confined space hot and sweaty with other human beings can create a level of discomfort not many of us face in our work; working in this same space with someone who has slopped his pigs and refuses to bathe is something we should really consider for torturing terror suspects.

He also would use his Coke uniform to slop his pigs and so in short order it was stained without a reasonable possibility of the stains ever being removed without scissors.

Finally, after a number of written warnings we terminated Brian and he left cussing and wild. I immediately asked the local managers to put some security personnel on premises.

You know sort of funny and kind of an aside, but when I think "security" I think of really big guys with really big guns and really big clubs who sort of stand around looking all big, menacing and stuff and don't smile at anyone. What I usually have seen, however, is retired Wal-Mart greeters who sometimes ride the bus to work because they've long since lost the ability to drive themselves with a gun on a belt hanging down around their knees; I think Schwarzenegger (think Terminator) and more often than not get Fife (think The Andy Griffith Show).

I know this is probably an unfair description, an unfair stereotype, but somewhere between my vision and my stereotype is what constitutes the security most companies provide and many times the security seems to be closer to my stereotype.

Grandpa slept at our front door for two weeks and at that time we decided Brian had run his course. I received an unemployment claim in the mail, responded to it and we won. We received a notice for a phone hearing and called the hearing officer at the designated time and Brian didn't call in and we won the phone hearing. He appealed and without further discussion we won again.

I spent several hours responding to his EEO complaint (age) and my attorney spent another couple of hours working on it and we sent it in. We didn't hear back from the EEO except when they sent us

☆☆☆☆☆
☆☆☆☆☆
☆☆☆☆☆
☆☆☆☆☆
☆☆☆☆☆
☆☆☆☆☆
☆☆☆☆☆

notification that Brian had not waited for the process to complete itself, but had asked for and received his "Right to Sue" letter. We next received a notice from the EEO (as I remember, but it may have been the court) for mediation and accepted and much to our surprise (that's why I think it was a mandatory court ordered mediation) so did Brian.

I flew in the night before the mediation. Our attorney flew in the night before as well. We met for some period of time (it seemed like an eternity, but was probably two to three hours) to discuss the "case." The following day we went to the mediator's office.

We were maybe fifteen minutes early. We waited. About thirty minutes later Brian walks in. The mediator admonished him for being late and received a response that could best be described as blank imbecilic. We sat down and the mediator began.

"This appears to me to be a fairly simple case without a lot of outstanding issues and I'd like to recommend we see where each side is at in this and begin our negotiation," she said.

Speaking to our counsel the mediator said "I'm going to sort of put you on the spot Mr. Alrod and ask you what Coca-Cola would be willing to settle this for."

"At best," Ernie began "and in our minds, this case has limited value and the value it has is of a nuisance nature. With that said, we'd be willing to offer up to one thousand dollars."

☆☆☆☆☆
☆☆☆☆☆
☆☆☆☆☆
☆☆☆☆☆
☆☆☆☆☆
☆☆☆☆☆
☆☆☆☆☆
☆☆☆☆☆

Even I thought Brian would jump at the chance to pocket a thousand dollars for nonsense.

The mediator turned to Brian. "Mr. Brumond is this the neighborhood in which you were thinking?"

Brian took a deep breath. "No mam." he said emphatically. "These sons a b_____ fired me for no reason and that's not anywheres close to what I was thinking. I want a million dollars."

"Excuse me?" the mediator asked.

"I want a million dollars," Brian said.

"Mr. Alrod?" the mediator slowly turned back to our attorney.

"I'm sorry, but as I said we're here to make a good faith offer of one thousand dollars, which we think is most fair, and we're not going to discuss anything higher."

"Mr. Burmond?" the mediator asked.

"I want a million dollars and that's final," Brian hissed.

The mediator turned to our attorney and then looked at me and smiled sort of plaintively and then turned back to Brian.

☆ ☆ ☆ ☆ ☆
☆ ☆ ☆ ☆ ☆
☆ ☆ ☆ ☆ ☆
☆ ☆ ☆ ☆ ☆
☆ ☆ ☆ ☆ ☆
☆ ☆ ☆ ☆ ☆
☆ ☆ ☆ ☆ ☆

"Mr. Brumond, I've read your complaint, the EEO complaint, the unemployment complaint. I've looked at the series of warnings you received and the company's policy regarding termination of employment and with all due respect I have to tell you how generous the offer of one thousand dollars seems to be as I have been doing this for a lot of years and you simply do not have a lot of ground to stand on."

Brian took another deep breath and then sprang to his feet, simultaneously slamming the palms of his hands down on the table sort of hopping up like a little mad troll. "By god," he said, "I want a million dollars and I'll accept nothing less from these sons a b_____." And with that he spun around, momentarily losing his balance but catching himself, and stormed out the door.

We all sort of looked at one another. "I think that concludes this mediation," the mediator said.

"Thank you" our attorney said and the stenographer began packing up her little machine.

I don't know if Brian thought "he'd been to court," or what, but we never heard another word from him.

(Yes, you read the preceding sentence right. To this day I do not know what happened to million-dollar Brian, but he never again graced our presence with his.)

☆ ☆ ☆ ☆ ☆
☆ ☆ ☆ ☆ ☆
☆ ☆ ☆ ☆ ☆
☆ ☆ ☆ ☆ ☆
☆ ☆ ☆ ☆ ☆
☆ ☆ ☆ ☆ ☆
☆ ☆ ☆ ☆ ☆
☆ ☆ ☆ ☆ ☆

I tell you this story to illustrate several salient points. I'll cover only one here. First and foremost, never hire a pig farmer murderer. Kidding, but really doesn't this story sort of remind you of one of those horror movies like *Leatherface: Texas Chainsaw Pig Farmer Murderer*?

What you'll find throughout this work, as well as some pretty powerful selection tools, is some basic common sense things that a lot of folks simply will not use. And each time they make a poor hiring decision they shrug their shoulders, complain about the applicant pool and blame the low wages the company is willing to start folks at and/or human resources. But they blow off the easy stuff.

We had to put our managers and other employees through the wringer as we had to ask the questions we felt the EEO and the plaintiff attorneys might ask. I did a lot of the leg work of our investigations and so spent several days interviewing and re-interviewing our managers and staff. We lamented a lot of missed opportunities to catch our erroneous hiring decision. I know our managers were worried and I know there were lots of sleepless nights. Our attorney wasn't a fan of our managers and possibly not much of a fan of me. The best way to advance a career is not by having a lot of employment claims and "noise" from your employees. By blowing off the easy stuff we probably spent around $15,000 to $20,000 exclusive of rehiring, re-training and lost productivity.

The following is an example of "easy stuff" that some folks don't use.

A letter of application and a resume is a picture of what the person applying wants you to see: The better the artist, the better the picture.

☆ ☆ ☆ ☆ ☆ _____ _____
☆ ☆ ☆ ☆ ☆ _____ _____
☆ ☆ ☆ ☆ ☆ _____ _____
☆ ☆ ☆ ☆ ☆ _____ _____
☆ ☆ ☆ ☆ ☆ _____ _____
☆ ☆ ☆ ☆ ☆ _____ _____
☆ ☆ ☆ ☆ ☆ _____ _____

My background is in technical communication with an undergraduate degree in English. I've been reading letters of application and looking at resumes for over twenty years. Do you think if I put together a letter and resume for a job that I have a better than even chance of someone looking at it and saying "hey, this guy looks pretty good?"

Nowhere in my resume does it talk about why I left my last job. I include limited information about start dates and end dates. It doesn't ask if I can prove I can work in the United States. It doesn't provide any information about my compensation even though new laws are making this ridiculous question something that can't be asked. Importantly, I don't sign anything saying "anything" or "everything" I've presented is true, or saying the company can check my background. And if a manager is comparing my resume to others, what criteria is he or she using to compare it?

"Well, Rex spelled everything right and John didn't and what's with that funky paper John is using anyway?"

As the run up to Obama, Clinton, McCain demonstrated and Clinton and Trump especially are re-demonstrating, the preceding may be criteria similar to what we use to elect presidents, but this sort of nonsense criteria shouldn't be the deciding factors in a hiring process for someone you actually have to work with (my dripping sarcasm is showing).

Resumes are like comparing apples to orangutans. You know there might be some similarities, like "they're each composed of energy," but you'd have to stretch to come to some meaningful comparison.

_____ ☆ ☆ ☆ ☆ ☆ _____
_____ ☆ ☆ ☆ ☆ ☆ _____
_____ ☆ ☆ ☆ ☆ ☆ _____
_____ ☆ ☆ ☆ ☆ ☆ _____
_____ ☆ ☆ ☆ ☆ ☆ _____
_____ ☆ ☆ ☆ ☆ ☆ _____
_____ ☆ ☆ ☆ ☆ ☆ _____
_____ ☆ ☆ ☆ ☆ ☆ _____

If your company doesn't have a formal application, find someone who can provide you with a copy of a legal one their company uses and copy it. You can also go "ask to apply" at some major employers, take their application, and be pretty certain you're going to see a legal application. You can go on to monster.com, careerbuilder.com, or indeed.com or do an internet search and find applications that usually will fit the bill.

The test I've used for eons for whether the query is "legal" on an application is "does it fit the job to be performed?" Generally marital status, birthday (you can ask "Are you over eighteen," but you should not [note the "should" and not "cannot;" you can ask anything, but I wouldn't] ask "How old are you," or get information that tends to indicate age like "date of graduation from high school"), religion, sex, disability, race, ethnicity, etc. should not be asked and you should try to find example, "legal," applications that shy away from these minefields.

I tell folks that there aren't "illegal questions" per se. You can ask someone how old they are, but unless you're hiring commercial jet pilots (which may be a little of a stretch) or astronauts (again, with John Glenn as a past example a stretch) I wouldn't because you probably can't use that information to determine if a person is qualified. You can ask if someone is Catholic, but if you're not hiring for a Priest or the Pope, I wouldn't ask whether someone is Catholic; it makes no sense as it has nothing to do with whether a person can do virtually any other job (even if you're hiring for an atheist newspaper, in my opinion, religion, or lack thereof, cannot legally be used as a hiring criteria). Maybe you're a Buddhist who happens to own a construction business and you "always try to hire Buddhists," which is fine and dandy, but there is nothing about being Buddhist that qualifies someone to hammer nails. And you can ask if someone is female, if you can't figure it out, if you're hiring for a midwife. Other than these limited examples you probably can't disqualify someone from hiring them based on any of the preceding attributes and a better question in a tight, and tightening, labor market would be "why would you want to disqualify people for nonsense?"

And, the application can still ask in most states what the ending compensation was at the person's last job. This can be valuable information. If you have a Customer Service Manager at your company and the position pays $16.50 an hour as its absolute top end, you probably don't want to consider the Customer Service Manager who is coming in and expecting a minimum of $27.50 an hour. Or, you might put a range for the position in your posting, if you don't want to ask this question, but I know some folks get "uneasy" with doing this because then "everyone knows."

At the same time don't disrespect and cheapen the hire, as virtually every company I've ever known does, by undercutting what you're willing to pay just because an applicant lowballs him- or herself. Pay what the job is worth to you if you are hiring a superstar because here in a moment I'm going to show you how to do that.

And, any definite information you might be able to check on provides you an opportunity not to "find someone who is lying," but simply to confirm information and make a good choice. The key is not to keep compensation "highly confidential," but to make it most fair.

☆☆☆☆☆
☆☆☆☆☆
☆☆☆☆☆
☆☆☆☆☆
☆☆☆☆☆
☆☆☆☆☆
☆☆☆☆☆
☆☆☆☆☆

Easy suggestion number one therefore is: Use a formal application and require everyone from the CEO on down to complete it before being considered for employment. And Easy suggestion number two, although it's probably Easy suggestion number "one A" is to require everyone in the organization who is hiring for a position to review the pertinent applications prior to interviewing someone.

And as an added bonus, if you want them, here are some things to look for when doing a quick review of the application:

Is it somewhat neat? This allegedly is the best an applicant can do. Even one that is filled out by hand should be legible with a lot of the junk on it spelled right.

Is it complete? Did the person follow the instructions? If the application says "You can attach a resume, but we still need you to complete the blanks under 'Employment History,'" did the applicant complete the blanks, or did he or she simply put "see resume?"

Maybe that's not a big deal, but more successful people understand instructions and how to follow rules. I've always tried to hire people with a rudimentary understanding of "rule following."

Are there gaps in employment history that make no sense? Are some of the dates illegible, or could the "6" be an "8," or a "5," or maybe the applicant "forgot" to put in a year. Be very careful. One "mistake" like this is a "maybe;" two and they're usually on my discard pile.

☆ ☆ ☆ ☆ ☆ _____
☆ ☆ ☆ ☆ ☆ _____
☆ ☆ ☆ ☆ ☆ _____
☆ ☆ ☆ ☆ ☆ _____
☆ ☆ ☆ ☆ ☆ _____
☆ ☆ ☆ ☆ ☆ _____
☆ ☆ ☆ ☆ ☆ _____

That may seem harsh, but I'm developing an impression from a cursory glance and that glance may seem harsh or unfair, but it is what it is and that glance can determine whether I'm stuck with someone for a very long time, so be careful and cautious and thorough, but also be highly, highly critical.

Did the person leave his or her last employer or last few employers for "political reasons," "didn't like my boss," or other reasons that indicate there was a problem with a relationship? Again, not a total disqualifier, but more successful people are able to build, grow and sustain relationships and you want to spend your time on productive things and not refereeing. People who moan and groan about previous employers will moan and groan about your organization as well—guaranteed.

Are there companies you can call to verify whatever limited information companies will give you nowadays, or are all the companies closed and where the application asks for a phone number is there none listed, or, again, could the "5" be a "6" or an "8," or possibly the number is in another area code and this information is "accidentally" missing? Put on your Inspector Gadget outfit and "Go, Go Gadget. Go." Ask a lot of questions not of every application, but of those you're seriously considering.

Is the person an adult? This is probably pretty hard to glean from an application and it has nothing to do with age, but if the person isn't an adult, you're sunk as you'll be messing with the children you've hired and not doing your job. And I will guarantee you there are those sitting there reading this right now with a wry smile on their face or gently nodding as they think of the children they've hired. Stop it. Hire adults. Work is an adult game; children can't play productively.

What's been their work history? Is there some indication of stability? Do there seem to be reasons for any apparent lack of stability? "Better opportunity" is usually a good reason for someone to leave, but going from $9.75 an hour to $7.16 an hour because "I got to be a manager" isn't a move up or a "better opportunity."

Look for these sorts of disconnects. And "Better opportunity" is great so long as those opportunities didn't come along three or four times in the last eight to twelve months. If they did then you are their next "better opportunity," but I will bet you dimes to donuts you're not the best.

Do they seem to fit the job? An MBA graduate applying for an entry-level accounting position may be okay, but check this out closely. A college graduate looking for a wait staff position is another one to look at. Don't exclude people because they look "over qualified," but definitely look hard at the qualifications. You want smart people in your organization, but be smart about it.

"Why does an MBA graduate who may have a whole bunch of doors open to her want to sell shoes in your store?" This may be a perfectly legitimate pursuit of a career if the person wants to learn "Brown Shoe Fit" from the bottom up and aspires to be the CFO or CEO one day, but be a little leery when the qualifications seem to far outstrip the needs. I'd rather hire an over qualified person and have him or her for a couple of years than to hire someone who takes two years to train them before I have to let them go (and of course I wouldn't advocate taking two years to train for most positions, but you get my point).

And Easy suggestion number two (or three if you count 1A as 2), and really my last one before getting into my Model, is don't hire just because you reach the bottom of the barrel and this one is the last one left. That's what we did when we found Brian. He was the last applicant left standing

and this shouldn't mean we hire him; if anything this probably means we shouldn't.

The rest of my book really talks about building a Model of what you're looking for and then continuing the hiring process until you've found the person that more or less fits the Model you will build.

So, strap on in and let's get started.

Chapter 4
Grabbing
The Ring

This Model building exercise is a revolutionary change.

Improving a process is generally evolutionary and over time (sometimes a short time) things can change dramatically.

Then you have revolutionary change: something so radical as to turn the world upside down. My Model may not be quite there, but, at a certain level, it's right on up there with "fire" and the "wheel" in terms of its ability to make a world of difference.

Sometimes when I look at the way many of us hire, I get this sense that we're in the dark ages, working out of our caves and just trying to find someone who won't hurt our chances for survival. That's not all bad as survival is a good thing, but moving our companies forward and in dramatic fashion in the lean years we've been in and the leaner years that may come is a much better way to survive (note: as you probably know as my Baby Boomer generation retires expect to see 20+ million or so positions that will not have people to fill them—the population numbers are not there—and, that's not even including the fact many of the people coming up don't have the skill sets we need).

☆☆☆☆☆
☆☆☆☆☆
☆☆☆☆☆
☆☆☆☆☆
☆☆☆☆☆
☆☆☆☆☆
☆☆☆☆☆
☆☆☆☆☆

Revolutionary change turned out to be a lot harder than I had envisioned. Here's why. Almost everyone, with even a couple of years of hiring experience, reading this, even though I'll repeat over and over several times the dramatic difference, is still thinking of "my Model" as some hybrid "job description." That's not a criticism. That's the power of what we're all so comfortable with, job descriptions.

Most of us are still thinking "hire the most qualified." And when we're thinking "qualified" where are we pulling the qualifications from?

The job description.

I don't even know what comparison to use to demonstrate how wrong this thinking is. It would be like looking for a problem with the prostrate by going through the mouth. Right general vicinity, but wrong entrance.

There's an excellent video on YouTube that shows our brain and how inflexible it is. In the search field on YouTube enter "backward brain bicycle." You're looking for this link, https://www.youtube.com/watch?v=MFzDaBzBlL0.

This is a video well worth the investment to watch. It truly boggles the mind. And so you know I had my son-in-law build me a backward brain bicycle and I brought it to work and about 50 people tried to ride it and everything, EVERYTHING, the video says is 100% accurate.

My Model is something akin to the backward brain bicycle. I'm not suggesting "job descriptions are all bad," although I believe they're quite challenged, but there's a different way to think about this hiring thing and if we take the time and build a Model rather than a job description, we can achieve phenomenal results.

Say you're looking for a new car. You need 4 wheels, an engine, an interior with seating, air conditioning would be nice, maybe something to entertain you, a steering wheel.

Are you shopping for an Accord or a Hummer?

Okay, let's attack the same question from a different angle.

If you're shopping for a car and you decide I want something that gets good gas mileage, is relatively comfortable, has sort of a sleek body and can move out pretty good when I punch the gas pedal.

Are you looking for an Accord or a Hummer?

That's the difference between a job description (first paragraph on cars) and my Model. My Model shows you specifically what you are looking for. If you're looking at a Hummer, but you know you need an Accord, the decision is easy.

Job descriptions are simply a listing of things that make up the car with limited thought given to what fits you and your organization, your team and most importantly your culture. Hire a Hummer when you need an Accord and you'll find you've created a wreck.

In this regard my Model is a revolution. The revolutionary change is you're getting rid of the notion of "job descriptions." In my opinion, they often don't work anyway, so the loss isn't that great.

With a Model you're not necessarily looking for the "best qualified." I'd argue we don't usually get that with a job description either. What we usually hire is someone who is most like us, but that's a different argument.

With my Model you're hiring someone closest to the fit you and your organization needs.

This is a big deal as survey after survey shows that "fit" is often times in the top couple of reasons people don't move an organization forward and also the reason they more often than not leave an organization. "Well, they just didn't 'fit.'"

A survey I ran had an interesting outcome. We were developing an on-boarding (new hire orientation) program. I wanted to see why people were leaving and the exit survey the company was using at the time wasn't complete junk, but, like many of these tools, it was pretty darned close.

We went back and talked with 18 months' worth of people who had terminated. Turns out they didn't leave for pay (well, a few), or poor

☆ ☆ ☆ ☆ ☆
☆ ☆ ☆ ☆ ☆
☆ ☆ ☆ ☆ ☆
☆ ☆ ☆ ☆ ☆
☆ ☆ ☆ ☆ ☆
☆ ☆ ☆ ☆ ☆
☆ ☆ ☆ ☆ ☆

supervision (some did), or because they did something wrong (a couple had). They left because they were afraid they might be doing something wrong.

Think about that one for a minute.

They left because no one was talking to them and simply telling them "you're doing okay."

That was sort of one of those mind boggling, unanticipated results. Without knowing exactly why people are leaving, determining how they will stay is a lot like throwing darts at a moving target with a blindfold on.

At Coke when we developed our on-boarding process we also ran an employee survey. The survey pointed to a lot of things we weren't exactly leading the pack on, but an interesting outcome was how incredibly tied to our logo, that little Coca-Cola swirl, our folks were.

They generally thought their supervisors were pretty poor with those of us in senior management leading this unenviable pack, their pay substandard and their working conditions horrid, but if we got them married to the logo, they stayed.

"You cut a Coke man and he bleeds Coca-Cola" is something we heard all the time from our employees. The survey confirmed it.

☆ ☆ ☆ ☆ ☆
☆ ☆ ☆ ☆ ☆
☆ ☆ ☆ ☆ ☆
☆ ☆ ☆ ☆ ☆
☆ ☆ ☆ ☆ ☆
☆ ☆ ☆ ☆ ☆
☆ ☆ ☆ ☆ ☆
☆ ☆ ☆ ☆ ☆

I built our on-boarding process and attempted to marry the newly hired employees to the logo. That was really its sole intent (outside of getting people to sign all the documents that explain how they get fired—what a stupid process that is—but, again, another time).

Did it work? I'm not a scientist. I don't know how to do a scientifically valid study. I trained about 100 people over about 9 months before the company sold and I left (or they left me to be more accurate). At the end of my tenure, the group I had trained (new hires) whose positions had been running in the 50% to 60% turnover range in their first 60 days of employment was running at 5.79% over the entire 9 months.

Our general population was running at about 37% turnover. Was it the on-boarding process marrying them to the logo, or was it just that they liked me...a lot? I don't know for certain, but I'll take those results anytime.

I'll use the following later in another chapter, but here are a few bullet points from a typical job description for a bank Teller:

- Primary function is performing various paying and receiving teller activities while providing excellent customer service with minimal balancing errors.
- Knowledgeable of the services and products offered by the Bank.
- May serve as back-up in the teller line as needed.

☆ ☆ ☆ ☆ ☆
☆ ☆ ☆ ☆ ☆
☆ ☆ ☆ ☆ ☆
☆ ☆ ☆ ☆ ☆
☆ ☆ ☆ ☆ ☆
☆ ☆ ☆ ☆ ☆
☆ ☆ ☆ ☆ ☆

- Provide customer service in a friendly, courteous and professional manner and represent the Bank, with a positive attitude.
- Knowledge of standard office equipment such as duplicating machines, telefax, laser printers, PC, and related software, such as Word for Windows, Excel and other EDS software or specialized accounting software.

Here's the first paragraph from a Model I built for the same position:

"Our Superstar CSR (Teller, which we renamed to Customer Service Representative) is first and foremost a customer service junky and a relationship building guru. These two traits came out over and over and over. In almost every answer customers were talked about. Even when I asked Tellers about the equipment that was most important to doing their job. "The computer because it speeds up transactions for our customers." Training? "I like training that lets me serve my customers better." Customer service was the focus of our most successful tellers. We can use this when we're selecting someone because we should get a real good sense of whether they believe in providing exceptional customer service. "

Now, hopefully, the difference between my Model and a job description is a bit clearer.

This Model defines what we are looking for and not a bunch of tasks that you put together and someone performs and they're magically an exceptional employee. A Model also takes the blindfold off and keeps

the target from moving. That's pretty good because we can throw in
the right direction, which is more than half the battle always.

What often happens in the hiring process is we receive ten or twelve or
a hundred or whatever resumes and/or applications. We then sit down
and start gleaning through the pile. Most of us approach this exercise
not looking for information to include someone, but looking for
information to exclude someone. The goal of this process is not to end
up with thirty-five potential interviews, but to end up with two or
three. Think about how you approach this process and see if the
preceding isn't a pretty accurate assessment—application/resume
evaluation is often a process of exclusion not inclusion.

To this end some of us look for what may constitute "little" things:
"misspellings," "sloppy handwriting," "a question missed." Some, too,
go to the totally arbitrary and occasionally borderline legal: "I don't
like that name," "his resume is too long," "why would someone use
beige paper?"

Whatever our selection criteria, generally speaking, our goal, again, in
the traditional hiring process is to par the list down to a manageable
number. "We haven't time for this junk."

In this regard, a Model makes a very subtle, but important change to
that process. We are still excluding the vast majority of folks, but we're
looking for the attributes from the Model that will allow us to include
someone. A Model, unlike a job description, allows you to include
people who actually are a fit to the needs you have. You may end up
with only two or three interviews still, but they'll be people who

genuinely have the capacity to outperform the rest of your workgroup and by a substantial margin. And, if you end up with 15 applicants, that doesn't mean you have 15 interviews; that means you sit down and sift the 15 down to three or four based off the "most qualified" when compared to your Model.

For example, our traditional Teller job description asked for "at least one year of Teller experience." Our Model talked about "money handling" experience. We didn't want someone absolutely green who had never felt other people's money running through their fingers, but we also didn't need someone with 14 years of Teller experience…necessarily. "Necessarily" because many times teaching an old dog new tricks truly is magnificently difficult and this "extremely qualified person" may turn out to be the last person you need in the long run.

Again, this flips standard logic on its head, but you're not looking for what you have.

You're looking for what you need, what you need to influence and transform your future, and this sort of "experience" may not be it.

Your Model will define the composite picture of your exceptional performers and then you will have the discipline to hire to your Model—to hire an exceptional performer.

The pool of prospective candidates widens geometrically when you define the skills and talents correctly.

☆ ☆ ☆ ☆ ☆
☆ ☆ ☆ ☆ ☆
☆ ☆ ☆ ☆ ☆
☆ ☆ ☆ ☆ ☆
☆ ☆ ☆ ☆ ☆
☆ ☆ ☆ ☆ ☆
☆ ☆ ☆ ☆ ☆
☆ ☆ ☆ ☆ ☆

Why?

Because you're no longer looking for "at least 1 year of Teller experience," or "3 years of direct sales experience;" you're looking for "money handling experience" (that's anyone whose run a cash register, worked in almost any retail, or quite possibly sold Girl Scout Cookies (although that is probably a stretch—the cookies, however, are great and therefore these people probably deserve to be looked at).

And what is sales? Yes, you absolutely positively have to find someone who is not afraid of the cold call and is more enthused with hearing "no" than any ten other people you know, but you also have to find that unique coupling of skills, talents and attitude that allow this person to also be the consummate relationship builder, a cornerstone of exceptional sales people.

The best way you can define the skills, talents and attitude you need is to ask someone who is inordinately successful in the role how the heck they achieve that great success. (BTW, you should five star this paragraph.)

There are, too, a host of managers who feel they can "motivate" their work groups to success. This is sort of true and sort of not. Usually we can generate some success with extrinsic motivation, but wouldn't a better approach be to hire motivated people? Oh, my. Think about that one for a minute. Would your work group look any different than it does today? Would your results be better or worse? Would you have a bookshelf that includes Bob Nelson's 1001 Ways to Energize Employees?

☆☆☆☆☆ _____
☆☆☆☆☆ _____
☆☆☆☆☆ _____
☆☆☆☆☆ _____
☆☆☆☆☆ _____
☆☆☆☆☆ _____
☆☆☆☆☆ _____

I find interesting this whole concept of motivation. For most managers when they want to make people move they offer money. Money is a great extrinsic motivator. But it isn't for everyone. Have you ever held a contest at work and told people "whoever gets to this point first wins and gets $150 (or whatever amount)?"

What happens in these sorts of contests is the person who is most comfortable doing whatever we ask to be done usually wins and the other folks sort of pretend to participate and act like "who needs $150?" The rest of the "losers," that's what they are, pretend to applaud the winner; over time, however, they're not all that happy as losers and they're not willing to expend the effort to become our definition of a winner, especially when being critical of the process, the unfairness of the contest, the arbitrariness of the organization and the stupidity of the boss is so much easier.

An employer I was working with once held a "wellness" contest. The winner would be the person who lost the most weight.

Never mind the argument about safe weight loss, or the argument that some people have more weight to lose than others, or the argument that weight isn't necessarily always a direct correlation to overall "health" (I'm not talking about obesity, but just folks who carry some extra weight and seem to manage it, health-wise, fine). Never mind the argument that generally speaking men can lose more weight faster than women. Never mind the argument that a pregnant woman should be under strict doctor's oversight if she decides to start reducing weight. Never mind that folks over 50 should consider the same "strict doctor's oversight" of the pregnant ladies.

☆ ☆ ☆ ☆ ☆
☆ ☆ ☆ ☆ ☆
☆ ☆ ☆ ☆ ☆
☆ ☆ ☆ ☆ ☆
☆ ☆ ☆ ☆ ☆
☆ ☆ ☆ ☆ ☆
☆ ☆ ☆ ☆ ☆
☆ ☆ ☆ ☆ ☆

The company was giving away a big screen television. One of the heavier people in the group of about 50 was a sports fanatic and wasn't in a position that afforded him a lot of discretionary income. First place was a big screen television. The Super Bowl was still months away. This kid was drooling at the opportunity. Everyone else thought it would be "fun." Everyone else, except the significant part of the population who thought "what business is it of this company how much I weigh?" Everyone else, except those who had maintained a healthy lifestyle and wondered what their reward was going to be knowing full-well their reward was "like it always is from these cheapskates...nothing!"

In short order he lost 180 pounds. He went from morbidly obese to anorexic in what seemed like days (it was actually a little less than four months, over a pound a day). The rest of the group lost some weight too until they saw they were up against "maniac weight loss dude" and then they gave up and watched stick boy as he continued to lose even when he started to look like one of those unfortunate starving children on the posters we see.

How did he lose all this weight? Did he reduce caloric intake? Did he exercise until he passed out? Did he take legal and illegal drugs? Did he purge after eating? Did he starve himself not even drinking water before each weigh in? Yes.

He did all the preceding things. He beat his body to death in every fashion ever devised to lose that weight and become more "healthful" and he won his television, set it up and 30 days before the Super Bowl he was watching his favorite sport shows on the weekends on his new big screen television. By Super Bowl day he'd gained back 45 pounds.

By the summer he'd put on another 100. July 4 rolled around and he was up another 20. By the end of the summer he'd put on another 60. And anyone adding the preceding numbers will quickly deduce that what came off in a rush as 180 pounds went back on in a flood as 225, 230, 235 pounds. When last I heard the incredible growing man was still growing. He was ready for the next weight loss contest though.

The point of this story is two-fold. First, all of us are motivated by different things. If we're not real good at the task being offered for reward, or the reward is not to our liking, we'll probably pretend, but we're sitting this one out. Second, we have to be careful of what we're rewarding. What does this have to do with hiring?

Because many of us never ask anyone anything. We have a sales contest and the winner gets $1,500. We have a sales contest and the winner gets a free trip. We have a…and the winner gets. We're motivating the person who is best at the task we're motivating (or is best at gaming the system, which happens all the time), or we're motivating the person most motivated by the reward. And maybe we have two or three of the preceding and so it looks like a contest.

I spoke with a friend of mine on a "sales" "team." He told me, and this was confirmed by another person on the team, that when "the boss" held these sorts of contests, there were four of the salespeople who would get together after work, decide who would be the "winners" and figure out how to split up the prizes. They'd been doing this for several years and it worked out great as they were able to maximize the prize money by directing the sales to the appropriate "contestant." And sometimes there was a clash because Ben and Charley both really wanted the trip, so they'd have to regroup when the wheels came off. They also kept this "team" together and didn't let new employees in to the point that these four were the sales core and other employees lasted only a few months. "You guys are my best," the manager would tell them. "You've been with me forever and you're always producing and I can't remember when someone other than one of you won the sales incentive. Remarkable."

At a distribution company I worked with they had a dizzying way of paying their route salespeople. The company knew that if the route salesperson grew his (they were all males) route beyond a certain point, he couldn't take proper care of the route. The company figured if the route salesperson was making around $30,000 a year the route was about the right size. But the company had salespeople growing their routes into the low $50s. The company knew the route salesperson couldn't possibly be taking proper care of his route, even though there was no evidence to suggest this, so the company would cut the route in half and give the excess to a new employee. The route salesperson's income went from $50,000 to $25,000 or $30,000 because he'd worked harder than everyone else and grown his route.

The route salesperson would grow it back and the company would cut it back again. The company would do this maybe twice and then the route salesperson would never grow his route above $35,000 to $37,000. The route salesperson knew that $37,000 was too small for the company to divide the route and although this wasn't $50,000 a year, $37,000 was better than working like a dog to grow the route to $50,000 and then as a reward be cut back to $25,000 or $28,000.

The company asked me to analyze why their best salespeople could no longer produce more after their first few years. After months and months and months of study and research (actually I always start with the compensation structure when the question is "why aren't salespeople producing" and I spent maybe half a day looking at this thing) I came up with the problem.

Senior management listened intently, were very receptive at "possibly looking at some alternatives," seemed genuinely interested as they looked at the alternatives and then went back to doing what they were comfortable with. They questioned "why," but couldn't accept the answer. Right now, to this day, well over 20 years later, I think the company still pays this same way and still gets the same results. I'm not sure if they've ever analyzed the problem again.

They never talked to the route salespeople about a more equitable system. I don't know what this company could have done in terms of sales if salespeople had been rewarded rather than penalized. The company's route volume probably would have looked a lot different.

We have to ask someone what it is that will take her from point A to point B. Then we have to put appropriate measures in place to monitor and allow the employee access to these measures so she can correct course. We also have to ask the person who is best at doing a particular job what made her so good at doing that particular job. Guessing ain't going to get us there and for crying out loud these folks

☆ ☆ ☆ ☆ ☆
☆ ☆ ☆ ☆ ☆
☆ ☆ ☆ ☆ ☆
☆ ☆ ☆ ☆ ☆
☆ ☆ ☆ ☆ ☆
☆ ☆ ☆ ☆ ☆
☆ ☆ ☆ ☆ ☆
☆ ☆ ☆ ☆ ☆

are our employees and we can ask them anything. This fear that some people have of "they'll get the big head" is nonsense and the only "big heads" I've ever been around at Coca-Cola, in banking or anywhere else are in senior management anyway. Maybe therein lies the problem.

What I noticed in this process of defining my Model is that supervisors are locked in their paradigms more rigidly than just about anyone because to get out of that paradigm threatens the way they've seen others, their mentors, become successful:

"I have this set of questions that has served me well for years."

"I know what I'm looking for when I find it."

"I've been doing this for eons and things are going along just fine."

"This whole hiring thing takes too much of my time already and now you're telling me I have to go spend more time? Have you completely flipped out of your gourd?"

I don't know a good argument to change the paradigm of supervisors. If there is one, I never found it. And that's not for "all" supervisors, but there's a pretty good percentage out there who we just have to work around, or get new supervisors. If you're in human resources, you already have this list even if it's just in your head. We all do.

☆ ☆ ☆ ☆ ☆ _____ _____
☆ ☆ ☆ ☆ ☆ _____ _____
☆ ☆ ☆ ☆ ☆ _____ _____
☆ ☆ ☆ ☆ ☆ _____ _____
☆ ☆ ☆ ☆ ☆ _____ _____
☆ ☆ ☆ ☆ ☆ _____ _____
☆ ☆ ☆ ☆ ☆ _____ _____

Senior management and ownership is the key to others buying into something new. Those groups and then add in supervisor compensation and bonuses tied to measurements like employee morale, productivity and retention and you'll see change.

In the training I developed for my Model, we did an exercise where I allowed supervisors to define the cost of turnover and I didn't even have to add the soft dollars and the cost of turnover came out always to between 0.75 and 2.5 times the cost of the position's annual compensation. Supervisors came up with this number. This was a great exercise and seemed to open a few eyes and turn a few heads. It wasn't a panacea, but I'd recommend a similar exercise. Let groups of these folks define how much it costs to lose someone and then let them present their findings to each other. The voyage of self-discovery can be a beneficial voyage indeed. And let them use the internet to search if you like. The internet often defines even more costs that we don't even think of.

In training, we also roleplayed and I had supervisors bring their tried and true questions and I built some scenarios of folks who they would be "interviewing" and then we went through the interview process and asked our questions and invariably they "hired" the ax murderer or the father rapist or the embezzler. This, too, was an exercise that opened a few eyes.

And every single supervisor I have ever trained has agreed with my core belief in terms of "the Model:" The Model employee, the exceptional performer, will out work the next best employee three, four…up to seven times to one. They even defined this part of the

☆ ☆ ☆ ☆ ☆
☆ ☆ ☆ ☆ ☆
☆ ☆ ☆ ☆ ☆
☆ ☆ ☆ ☆ ☆
☆ ☆ ☆ ☆ ☆
☆ ☆ ☆ ☆ ☆
☆ ☆ ☆ ☆ ☆
☆ ☆ ☆ ☆ ☆

exercise by thinking about the best employee they ever had and laying out what benefits this sort of employee brought to the manager when compared to others on their staff.

What they all agreed to was that the exceptional employee will produce up to seven times as much "humph" as the next best performer, they don't require much supervision, they're dependable and they're generally pleasant to be around with few personal problems.

But reality is a really rough thing. A supervisor spends a few hours with me, takes her 3-ring binder with all the questions and answers and theories and research in it, takes the PowerPoint slide presentation and the Excel worksheets and goes back to her office with access to everything in PDF. She lays the 3-ring binder with its associated materials neatly displayed behind the nicely typed tabs on her desk. A few weeks after she's done this she places the binder in her bookshelf, possibly on its side as it's too high for the shelf.

A couple of weeks or months later, a position comes open, she pulls the job description, pulls out her list of tried and true questions, does her 20 minute interview, and hires the "best qualified" who looks and acts remarkably like the manager.

"Sorry, Rex, I simply didn't have time to go through the process this time, but I will next. Next time I'm going to use our Model because I really think the concept has merit."

The best motivator I've found for supervisors is two-fold. First, if we expect people to take the time then we need to give them the time. That means hiring the support they need to do the job right. Or, providing them the support to do the job right. How about a hiring SWAT team that goes in with "a manager" to take the manager's place and the manager works with the rest of the SWAT team and develops and hires to a Model?

Second, managers must be held accountable for the results their people achieve and the results they achieve managing their people. Period. End of discussion. Managers' jobs, at least those managers charged with managing people and not processes, are to get results through people. If a manager runs 134% turnover, hires the first person who can pee and fog up a mirror and doesn't use the tools the organization provides to correct the problem, that manager needs to be held accountable. If the manager perpetually will not listen, blames his turnover for his poor results and seems to be running a zoo of insane cockroaches rather than a workgroup, that manager needs to be held accountable.

This accountability can be the negative consequence of discipline ("discipline" for adults in our workplace; what a concept, but another argument for another time for another piece, just know I hate this concept; it's ridiculous—discipline and adults--ridiculous), or the positive consequence of reward (which can, unfortunately, when used incorrectly be as detrimental as discipline).

The coveted bottom-line, however, is there are a lot of managers out there who cannot manage and don't need to be. It's not "their fault;"

they were the one sitting there with the most tenure and so we promoted them. Tenure and the fact someone can do the job they're currently in is not "a model" for managing people—"gets results through others" may be a piece of this sort of model.

I had the opportunity to experiment with several managers over the course of a number of years. One of these managers, I'll call him Dan, was a hotshot, go-getter from the word "now." We always had a great relationship and Dan was just smart enough to be a constant positive challenge.

"Rex," Dan called excited one day. "I have two great candidates and I want you to look at their applications and tell me which you would hire."

One applicant was "Steady Eddie." He had been in the same job in a warehouse (which is the job we were hiring for) for twelve years. The company was moving and his job was being eliminated and he was looking for work. Not flashy. Just there every day; doing the job. The other was "Dan junior," my manager, less 15 years. A hotshot, go-getter with more energy than a humming bird. His application showed he hadn't found his niche yet and his last three jobs had lasted for a combined total of just a few months more than two years (less than a year each).

I talked with manager Dan. "I'd go with Steady Eddie if I were you, Dan. He'll be there for the long run." This was a warehouse job. It didn't require flash or glamour. It required "Steady Eddie."

☆ ☆ ☆ ☆ ☆
☆ ☆ ☆ ☆ ☆
☆ ☆ ☆ ☆ ☆
☆ ☆ ☆ ☆ ☆
☆ ☆ ☆ ☆ ☆
☆ ☆ ☆ ☆ ☆
☆ ☆ ☆ ☆ ☆

"But the sales guys are chomping at the bit for me to hire the other guy and so that's the way I'm leaning," Dan explained. A lot of our salesforce started in the warehouse and worked their way into sales. Technically, we didn't often hire "warehouse" people, we hired salespeople who didn't mind biding their time in the dungeons of our warehouses.

"He won't be there a year," I said.

"Will to," Dan shot back. "In fact I'll bet you a steak dinner he's here past his one year anniversary."

I laughed. "Okay, you're on."

The steak was really good. Dan and I talked over the phone. He hadn't hired what he needed. He hired someone he perceived the organization needed and that was fine and a worthwhile goal, but the kid hadn't found his niche and there was nothing to suggest our company was it.

To add insult to injury the kid, knowing of our wager, quit without notice the day before his one year anniversary. He was sending a loud and clear message to Dan related to Dan's management style. Dan and I talked some about that as well. What the kid who left without notice didn't know is I've never won a bet and so I paid for the steak dinner with Dan. As the head of Human Resources we shouldn't win these sorts of bets and we should make them only as a friendly "wager" and not as an "I won. Pay up."

☆ ☆ ☆ ☆ ☆
☆ ☆ ☆ ☆ ☆
☆ ☆ ☆ ☆ ☆
☆ ☆ ☆ ☆ ☆
☆ ☆ ☆ ☆ ☆
☆ ☆ ☆ ☆ ☆
☆ ☆ ☆ ☆ ☆
☆ ☆ ☆ ☆ ☆

I had a manager who had the highest turnover rate in our company. His goal in life was to make more money than Ross Perot (Gates was just on the horizon at the time). I told him that for every one percent he reduced his turnover rate, I'd pay him $1,000 up to $10,000 and I'd pay him the portion of the bonus based on monthly results. The whole formula was a little more complicated, but this was a sales guy used to complicated formulas and also driven by cash. He maxed out his $10,000 before the end of the third quarter and never went back to the turnover rate he had.

As it turned out he started running all sorts of contests with his crew and each contest was dependent on people being there and he was running contests where he gave away dinner for two, or one part of a foursome for one of the many golf tournaments our company was involved in. He also quit yelling at them and started helping them achieve their goals. He used to just think he could run through people until he found that "natural born salesperson," but now he was coaching them, or doing what he thought was coaching which was really more like less intense cajoling, and taking someone who had the aptitude and building on that.

He did keep a couple of folks that we really should have let go, so I made a mental note to modify the incentive should I ever use it again. This manager went from a turnover rate of around 87% to a turnover rate of less than 10%. And at the end of that year, we gave him a raise equal to this "turnover/retention" bonus of the previous year and we conditioned his keeping it and his job for that matter on his maintaining the retention results he had. He never went backwards and his turnover rate actually improved slightly. By the end of the third year of

☆ ☆ ☆ ☆ ☆ _____
☆ ☆ ☆ ☆ ☆ _____
☆ ☆ ☆ ☆ ☆ _____
☆ ☆ ☆ ☆ ☆ _____
☆ ☆ ☆ ☆ ☆ _____
☆ ☆ ☆ ☆ ☆ _____
☆ ☆ ☆ ☆ ☆ _____

this process his team was the top producing group in the southwest region of the company and he was at the top of the retention list.

There were times like this where things happened with managers that made revolutionary change a bit easier to sell. There were times, too, that revolutionary change or not wouldn't have mattered in the least.

We were losing a ton of product from our northern warehouse. I spoke with the senior managers and we installed some hidden cameras. A few weeks later we had our man, Stephen, a 17-year junior manager, who was carting off product in his pickup on Sunday nights.

I called this manager's supervisor, Mark, and explained what we had. Mark was livid. A 35-year company man with years and years of experience I thought he was going to kill Stephen as Mark had hired and mentored him since Stephen had come on board.

We fired Stephen after an investigation that had him finally admit he was the culprit. He said his brother had gotten into trouble with some loan shark and he was selling our product on the black market to keep his brother from being killed. I couldn't disagree with the stated goal, if true, but of course we couldn't keep him either.

After this meeting Mark asked me into his office. He began to cry. I find watching a man cry, much less one who was about my father's age, difficult at best. He was questioning everything about himself. He knew Stephen. He'd hired him. He'd taught him everything. He, Mark, must be about the worst manager I'd ever run across he said.

Actually I assured him he wasn't even in contention for that award. I told him basically "stuff happens." I asked him how many other poor hiring decisions he'd made. After initially saying he wasn't sure he admitted that Stephen was his first. When I said "Stephen gave us 17 great years and then made a really bad decision. Do you think as a manager you should have been able to see into the future 17 years?" Mark began to understand that all the hiring tools in the world won't prevent reality crashing down on occasion.

The Model will allow you to hire much better people, but there's nothing perfect out there to hire perfectly every time and there's not anything in the world that will predict that should someone get between a rock and a hard place he or she doesn't make the decision to get out from under that predicament by penalizing your company. There just isn't.

The Model gives you the best chance of success I've ever found. Hiring the way I've described earlier, the way most of us hire with a list of questions and a job description puts us averaging a great hire well less than 10% of the time (remember from Chapter One, the statistic I quoted was talking about a satisfactory hire 10% of the time—I'm talking about hiring barn burners). I've found behavior-based interviewing done really, really carefully can push that number of satisfactory hires to anywhere from 30% to 50%. A Model will push that further to 80% and easily above. If you add some behavioral testing on top of that we can go up even further, although I might argue that as you start pushing the 90% window, although I've been sitting at 100% exceptional performers, knock on a forest, with my last dozen or so hires, the definition of "great" has to be a little suspect.

☆☆☆☆☆ _____
☆☆☆☆☆ _____
☆☆☆☆☆ _____
☆☆☆☆☆ _____
☆☆☆☆☆ _____
☆☆☆☆☆ _____
☆☆☆☆☆ _____

That's about as good as this deal gets, but that's not bad as long as you're not hiring airline pilots or cardiologists. 9 out of 10 is better than 5 out of 10 anyway and when you're hiring something as dynamic and clever as the human animal, 9 out of 10 is perfection.

Talk with senior management about holding managers accountable for using my Model. Accountability through positive reinforcement is usually an easier sell and is definitely longer lasting and is absolutely more "adult" and consequently enormously more respectful. Tell them to try this Model process for three to five years. If the results don't happen, you're still hiring better people because you're using a much more advanced behavior-based selection process.

I recently had lunch with one of the managers I used to work with. She went through my training many years ago, was an exceptional manager to begin with and about six or seven years after the fact still swears by my Model. Those are the sorts of recommendations that have substance.

If senior management thinks holding managers accountable for failure to use a Model, or rewarding folks for their retention (don't figure in involuntary terminations, retirements and deaths) rates, is a bad idea, and if they won't seriously pony-up to the table and pay for training even to the point of bringing in a so-called expert like me to kick off the effort, then you've read hopefully some good information and maybe you've gotten some ideas out of it that you can use, but you're probably not going to make a revolutionary change in your company.

☆ ☆ ☆ ☆ ☆
☆ ☆ ☆ ☆ ☆
☆ ☆ ☆ ☆ ☆
☆ ☆ ☆ ☆ ☆
☆ ☆ ☆ ☆ ☆
☆ ☆ ☆ ☆ ☆
☆ ☆ ☆ ☆ ☆
☆ ☆ ☆ ☆ ☆

Chapter 5
Stopping the
Merry-Go-Round

The following is easily the most important part of this work. Stopping the Merry-Go-Round is about Model Design sets up the next chapter, Selecting The Ring. Both are foundational to hiring the right person. And understanding how this works is more about working with it over time than about reading this chapter and the next and charging out there and building Models, although understanding this concept is probably as much doing as not, so prepare to charge, or potentially more accurately muddle, ahead.

Please know the muddling becomes clearer and clearer until building Models becomes extremely natural.

And, there'll be some overlap between this chapter and the next. That's okay, but be a little forewarned that you may read something in the coming pages that sounds very familiar in the next chapter where I present the example Model I'm discussing in the following.

This whole concept of Model building reminds me of the concept of "paradigm." A lot of people know what paradigm means: "a model," or "how we view the world." Both these are accurate and both are wholly inadequate. The second definition, "how we view the world," probably comes more closely to a working definition than "a model," but without a significant exercise in very deep thinking understanding the sheer power of paradigms is an impossibility. Without this "exercise in deep thinking" paradigm remains a funny little word, an enigma, meaning "a model."

That's probably a reasonably poor example of the power of this whole "Model" concept. The reason being is that most folks are not any closer to understanding paradigm than they were before they read the preceding paragraph and, therefore, the allusion I was attempting to make probably fell well short of its intended mark.

Suffice to say I believe my Model is the single most important element in our ability to hire the right person the first time. Hopefully that alone will lead to understanding that this chapter is less about reading and more about study, thinking and doing.

I first met Susie as you meet most applicants, during the interview. She was a quiet, but a quietly energetic person and I was immediately taken by her quick wit and obvious intellect. I was already forming an opinion of how she would interact with my other workaholic, Esther, and starting to formulate ideas I had for her going forward.

Whereas my current assistant, Esther, was, at the time, the hardest worker I'd ever been around, Susie was one of the smartest. Susie had everything that Esther lacked including a lot of computer skills, something I was having to help Esther with from day one. I was excited, put together a promising offer and called Susie.

☆ ☆ ☆ ☆ ☆
☆ ☆ ☆ ☆ ☆
☆ ☆ ☆ ☆ ☆
☆ ☆ ☆ ☆ ☆
☆ ☆ ☆ ☆ ☆
☆ ☆ ☆ ☆ ☆
☆ ☆ ☆ ☆ ☆

Without hesitation she accepted the position. She started a short time later and we never looked back. It was a spectacular hiring decision. When Esther's husband transferred, Susie came to me and asked if she could try to absorb benefits as well. I told her she could try, but I didn't want her to drown or get burnt out. Her hours increased to about 45 per week and she handled both areas flawlessly, almost effortlessly. I paid her more than I had ever paid anyone in my career and she was worth every dime. And yet I knew, especially as a company grows, there is always a problem whenever you have someone in a position controlling so much.

I hired Dora as an administrative assistant to take some of the load off and Susie was fine with it and seemed to like the company and didn't seem to mind the help. Slowly, I asked Susie to cross-train Dora, so that when Susie left on vacation, Dora could "take care of things." There were some fits and starts to this process as Susie's expertise and competence pretty much overwhelmed Dora, but eventually we had cobbled together a semi-working solution.

A few years later Susie, my superstar, came into my office and she was leaving. She wanted to pursue a different career, always had, and was moving on. Over the next several months she helped me out repeatedly as I had to train and retrain Dora and we had some bumps, bangs and crashes here and there.

Susie helped me out, too, in fleshing out and finalizing the idea of this "Model" concept. I knew I wanted to hire someone exactly like Susie. I had hired almost perfectly to my weaknesses and she filled in every gap. I wanted to have her personality, competence and aptitude down on a sheet of paper where I could compare her against all future applicants. I had used a testing service in the past to analyze people's areas of strength and determine what resources they would need to succeed.

I called Rod and he ran a battery of math, English and personality profiles on Susie. Rod and I talked about the results.

"Rex," Rod said, "it's admirable you want to hire someone like Susie as she's real special, but…"

There's always a "but."

"…but, you're probably not going to find another Susie, in terms of math aptitude, in Lubbock, Texas."

"Oh, really," I said, "and why is that?"

After a moment's hesitation Rod said "because she's in the top four percent nationally in terms of her math aptitude."

And then it hit me. The reason we had been so successful together. Susie was a perfect complement to a major area of concern I had in my personal array of talents. I was real good at manipulating numbers. One of the reasons I learned Excel backwards and forwards was because it allowed me to make numbers dance. This allowed me to take almost any set of financials and manipulate them into whatever bar chart, pie graph, pivot table, or whatever I, or another (usually the CFO, my boss) wanted.

But I didn't have, and never have, a true aptitude for math. I can do with words what CFO-types can do with numbers. I can take a paragraph of text and discern what it is the author is trying to say and with some effort massage that paragraph into something well beyond coherent and well beyond simply readable. When I do this right, I produce something almost musical.

People with an aptitude for numbers can do something like that with numbers. That's something, as hard as I might try, I will never be able to do. This is a limitation most of us have as we didn't train our brain to allow us that much flexibility—we can't "do hard science" and "do soft science" simultaneously. With Susie, I could make the numbers sing through her and, most importantly, she could explain what the symphony meant.

That's what I wanted to hire.

Dora, my other assistant, came to me and wanted "the" position (of course). I explained that I was either hiring a Payroll person or a Benefits person because I felt the load was too great and we needed two (I didn't tell her that I didn't think she could handle the load of the two positions—in my mind she wasn't Susie) and she could have whichever she wanted. I failed to be honest with Dora and tell her there was no way in my mind she could succeed.

She pleaded and pleaded and I finally acquiesced and allowed that she could "test" for the position and so I ran her through the battery of tests to see how aligned with Susie she was. I figured that then I would have definitive "proof" and could sit and show Dora where she lacked what Susie had and why she would not succeed.

Here's what I learned. Be honest, deathly, painfully honest. I wasn't and it cost me. Watch.

I was the one who was surprised. When I received the test results back Dora's scores lined up favorably with Susie's. None of them were as high, but she still had strength in math aptitude, was a bit weak in English and carried a "can do" attitude.

Think of a bell-shaped curve, but the bottom of the curve, on the left side, is at the eightieth percentile and the far right of the curve is up somewhere in the stratosphere of the ninetieth percentile. This was Susie's, the person who was leaving, bell-shaped curve. Then if you superimpose Dora's over the top of it, her left hand side of the curve was in the sixty-fifth to seventieth percentile and her upper limit was in the mid-eightieth percentile.

Confused? Well the bell-shapes were almost twins and there were just 10 or 15 percentage points that separated them and I kept hearing Rod's voice in my head "you're probably not going to find another Susie, in terms of math aptitude, in Lubbock, Texas."

I made the decision to allow Dora to try. To say this was a disaster would probably be a little dramatic, but to say it was one of my fairly decent ideas would definitely be giving me credit where none is due.

Important lesson number one about Models. Write this down as it's way, way important: *A little means a lot.*

Be careful if you're using a scale that is an empirical measurement. A swing of eight or nine points may not seem like a lot, but the difference between the king (or queen) of the hill and the rest of the heap is often a matter of a few degrees on these sorts of scales. The difference between the king (or queen) of the hill and the rest of the heap, however, in terms of a Model is gigantic.

You want to try and hire the king (or queen) of the hill, or someone as close to that proximity as is reasonably possible to find. If a major function of the job requires "math aptitude," then hiring below the level you need, will geometrically exacerbate the problems you face.

That last sentence of that last paragraph is an analogy to numbers and math aptitude and I'm not even sure what it means, but it sounds really bad. It sounds really bad because it is.

Important lesson number two about Models: *You have to know what you need before you go find it.*

Usually when we start to build a house we go out and find someone with a hammer, give her a big pile of wood and a sack of nails and say "knock yourself out," right?

Right?

Of course not. There has to be a plan doesn't there? We have to know, for example, how big the rooms are going to be, where the electrical and plumbing goes, how high the walls are and what color the carpet going up the stairs is.

We have to have a similar plan in hiring as well. I'm going to use a term here to get people thinking in roughly this direction, but I don't want folks to vomit either, so when I say the following I'm referring to something much more bold and creative, then the vomit-inducing terminology I'm about to use: job description.

I'll pause a bit because I know even with my forewarning there are folks who have vomited and won't return for a little while.

Okay, everyone back? Job descriptions were the bane of my existence in human resources; I rank them right up there with those gosh awful, terrible, despicable performance appraisals. I once asked a labor law attorney, who was longer in the tooth than me, if he had ever seen a company perform a decent performance appraisal. He had been practicing labor law for over thirty years, he'd been in court hundreds of times, he probably had seen just about everything there was to see in regards to "labor law." He responded "once I had a client that did 'okay' with them." And then added "and they were just decent." Then he added, "of course they didn't actually use a formal one, just talked with employees on occasion about the job they were doing."

I've never seen a performance appraisal system I think is worth using and I've never seen a job description that's worth writing. That doesn't mean they don't exist and that doesn't mean your company's appraisal system or job description process is not just the best thing ever. What that means is I have a strong bias against such things and haven't ever used one I like (although I built a performance appraisal at a bank I worked with that was amazingly, incredibly short and if you have to use one, I'd advocate go with something like "Is this person performing: Yes/No?").

Job descriptions became very hot topics after the ADA (*Americans with Disabilities Act*, July 26, 1990) because these job descriptions allegedly would show what physical capabilities were necessary to perform what elements of what jobs.

An attorney at a company I briefly consulted with hired an intern (some kid working on his master's) and he ran around the company for an entire summer building these "ADA compliant" job descriptions that would have been humorous, but they cost the company a small fortune and folks who we were hiring almost universally thought they were silly and those who didn't were just being polite.

And they were silly as they delineated the "Essential Functions" into parts that could have been definitions, stark examples, of irrelevant minutia and with every part there was an accompanying "physical requirements" that simply raised the everyday physical contortions we all go through to perform our jobs to a marquee level not deserved.

A Model is based on the essential elements of the job, but that's where the comparison to a "job description" pretty much ends.

A merchandiser of soft drink products in a traditional job description will have a task that reads something like the following: "Will merchandise store shelves, insuring no out-of-date product, insuring product is faced and insuring shelves are clean."

An element for a Model this same supervisor in the soft drink industry will be evaluating during a behavioral interview might be "Will insure customer satisfaction."

I don't want to be mean or make anyone upset with my disdain for job descriptions. So if you read the following and just absolutely hate the analogy, move on to the next section and don't worry about it. This is simply a picture into the recesses of my brain and they sometimes scare me.

A job description treats us like the basketball playing chicken. That's an analogy to an old carnival-type "game" that PETA (People for the Ethical Treatment of Animals) probably has, and should have, eliminated from most of the planet. At a carnival, the county fair, when I was a kid, off to the side there was always this glass cage with a chicken in it and at one end was a little basketball goal. You dropped money in the slot and a bell and light went off and a little basketball appeared and the chicken would beat itself to death until it pecked that

☆☆☆☆☆
☆☆☆☆☆
☆☆☆☆☆
☆☆☆☆☆
☆☆☆☆☆
☆☆☆☆☆
☆☆☆☆☆

little ball into that little hoop. When the chicken succeeded the bell would sound and the light would go off and a bunch of food pellets would drop out of a chute and the chicken would go gobble up the food. You could do this a hundred times in a row and the basketball playing chicken would grab the product, face the product and make sure the shelves were clean. Every time.

In other words a job description could be used to teach someone a new trick. And I'm not suggesting a Merchandiser or anyone else is a basketball playing chicken, but eventually I've seen these good, intelligent people in these sorts of positions simply walk away and we can drop all the quarters we want in the slot, but the only thing that will happen is the basketball will pop out, roll around and come to a stop. We have to engage, especially with the younger generations, people's brains, but more importantly we have to engage their hearts.

"I want you to merchandise store shelves, insuring no out-of-date product, insuring product is faced and insuring shelves are clean" may not accomplish this goal. "I want you to do whatever it takes within the confines of honesty, good morals and good ethics, to satisfy this customer" comes a heck-uv-a-lot closer. Then, we train the details.

A Model elevates us to using our hearts and brains. What my Model focuses on is the elements of a job that make the most successful individuals do that job successful.

Almost every job, including Merchandiser of soft drinks, is going to be dependent on others. Therefore, I am assuming an integral part of the Merchandiser's success will be "Relationship building." A sub-element under this might be "Will insure customer satisfaction." Or, on further investigation, this element might be a dominant element we want to focus on. But how do we know?

I saw a young kid run around a company all summer and build a handful of well-thought-out, very detailed job descriptions that for most supervisors went in the trash except when the General Counsel was around. The effort it takes to put together a reasonable proximity of a Model for a specific position is greater; the return on investment, however, is astronomically higher.

Let me back up and explain the process a bit and then explain why it's worth the efforts.

(And, yes I know there are folks who want to "get going." Here's my advice. Please read the rest of this chapter. The interview questions and process I use to build a Model for supervisors and employees are sprinkled throughout this chapter and the following chapter is essentially one of the Models I built and have modified/perfected over time.)

The Model is not a description of the position; it's a composite picture of the most successful candidates in a position.

Digest that for a moment, if you will, because that is a seriously huge difference. The tendency when we go into this process is to be predisposed by what we think a position looks like and to go in thinking "we need to do a task analysis." Do that and you fail in in building a Model.

☆ ☆ ☆ ☆ ☆
☆ ☆ ☆ ☆ ☆
☆ ☆ ☆ ☆ ☆
☆ ☆ ☆ ☆ ☆
☆ ☆ ☆ ☆ ☆
☆ ☆ ☆ ☆ ☆
☆ ☆ ☆ ☆ ☆

One of my most complete Models, a position I fully defined, was for a bank and was something of a more involved test of my theory: Teller (the next chapter is more or less a facsimile of what this Model looks like, although where I started and what the next chapter represents are about as different as different gets). I knew quite a bit about tellers, not from having been one, but from hanging around and watching and listening to them interact with customers and…and…from reading the job description.

I knew from the job description that there were several things I would be including in their Model as pre-conditions for employment. The job description said that "ten-key by touch was 'strongly' preferred." A ten-key is the numeric keypad on many computer keyboards with zero at the bottom and 1 through 9 above in rows of three. "Ten-keying" was the ability to add, subtract, multiple and divide using this numeric keypad. And like typing by touch, "ten-key by touch," meant someone would not even be looking at this numeric keypad. Ten-key by touch is a pretty significant trick.

I knew there were companies who could test, pre-employment, for ten-key proficiency. I knew from the job description that "computer skills" were required; I knew from watching that every teller spent a lot of time keying stuff into a computer terminal, so I had confirmation that this was an essential skill a teller needed prior to employment.

I knew from the job description that "a high school graduate or someone with demonstrated math skills 'to four digits' and a basic understanding of decimals, percentages and fractions" was required.

☆ ☆ ☆ ☆ ☆
☆ ☆ ☆ ☆ ☆
☆ ☆ ☆ ☆ ☆
☆ ☆ ☆ ☆ ☆
☆ ☆ ☆ ☆ ☆
☆ ☆ ☆ ☆ ☆
☆ ☆ ☆ ☆ ☆
☆ ☆ ☆ ☆ ☆

I knew these things because I'd read them over and over and over again even in the couple of handfuls of job postings I'd already done after joining the company. So, I also knew on the front-end of this "building my Model process" there were empirical things I would absolutely, positively test for.

A funny thing though happened on the way to my assumptions as facts got in the way.

To get to this composite Model I'm talking about requires discarding what we think a job is and thinking about what makes a person successful in that role because a job isn't a bunch of tasks we cobble together and when all the steps are followed in order we suddenly have the magic of a job being performed the way it should be performed.

The symphony, the seemingly effortless beautiful music that fills the room with their every motion, comes from the person we put into that job.

A successfully performed job is as much the result of the person in the job as it is in how we define the role.

Important lesson number three about Models. *Lose your paradigm of "jobs" and adopt Southwest Airlines' philosophy: "Hire for Attitude and Train for Skill."*

I would suggest that you're not wanting to hire the happy, go-lucky, kid who won't tie his shoes, or tuck in his shirt, or simply because he has a positive attitude, but you're hiring a person who will be a part of a team, who will interact with your customers, who will drive the success of your business.

To this point Southwest Airlines hires extremely competent pilots, but they also work to hire pilots who fit on their time and within their organization.

Just try putting a grump in any position, try putting the Grinch, pre-transformation after meeting the little Who, in any position and see what results you get.

And there are a lot of folks who just read that and said "No kidding!" "Hire for Attitude and Train for Skill" is the single greatest paradigm (the way we view things) shift that most managers can never achieve as they prefer to hire "the most qualified candidate."

Problem is the supervisors are defining "most qualified" based on, yep, the job description. And who cares if the basketball playing chicken is grumpy?

To get to this composite I'm talking about requires interviewing a select group of the company's exceptional performers in the specific role (if there's only one, do what I did with Susie and get as much information through empirical testing and lots and lots of conversations as you can). Then, interview their managers. Please note too I did not use "top" as in "top performers." An exceptional performer and a top performer are often times one in the same, but just because someone gets to a goal does not make them exceptional.

You're looking at the process of how they achieved their goals. When a composite picture is established through this investigative process, it's confirmed by one or two or more interviews and then the process stops and further development of a Model begins.

As I mentioned I decided my first gigantic shot out of the bag in terms of this whole Model thing would be tellers. I was working at a bank at the time. They weren't that interested in my concept, but they were okay with me "playing" around with this "idea" and if something came out of it of value, they wouldn't mind using my work, so I brought in research I'd been doing for years and years, and started with my already well developed concept and this agreement with them and that was fine by me.

The proof, for me, has always been in the proverbial pudding. I wasn't building this idea for this bank after all; I had started months and years before I was even working there and most the theoretical work was done. I was building this to see if indeed I'd stumbled on a solution to the age old dilemma of finding the right person, using a scientific method.

The catalyst in fact had nothing to do with my paid work. Many years ago I was volunteering for a major not-for-profit when the Executive Director tendered her resignation. We were devastated. The organization turned to me and asked me, the human resources/hiring guru, to help hire the next leader. I brought together all my hiring consultant notes and matrices and forms. I gathered a small team of HR professionals and business professionals. We vetted the job description, adding, subtracting, adding some more, subtracting some more. We hammered and hashed out the interview questions, built a scoring matrix for the resume, application, letter and interview. We posted the job, received the applications, closely screened the applications and began the interview process.

Based off the science of a very involved matrix, we winnowed the field down to three. We held second interviews. We called a firm to administer some "tests." We performed background checks.

We hired.

Within six weeks we started the process over.

We hired badly.

Sound familiar?

Somewhere following the result in the preceding I made a conscious decision to finish the work I had begun four or five years earlier and figure out this hiring mystery. I already knew "consultants" weren't the answer (I'd tried them and although they bring something to the table, it's not "mine" and it's not "the" answer and, although there are a ton of really good, really caring consultants, they have no stake in the company).

I had tried "behavioral interviewing" and my lawyers were super-happy with the copious notes I generated, although I absolutely dreaded the excruciating hand pain following one of these behavioral interviewing marathons. I did, however, have better results with "behavior interviewing" than with the "can they fog up a mirror?" employment test. But I was missing something. I made a decision to find out what.

My Model is the "what" I found.

I read a ton of books on turnover, retention, motivation, management and hiring, and a ton more on successful companies. This was in addition to the library of work I had started reading from the outset of my career in human resources. And I'm not saying this so folks can say "gosh that Rex must sure be smart," although if someone wants to say that I'm okay with it. I'm saying this so people know I don't believe in reinventing the wheel and so they don't think I woke up one morning with the thought "I think the way to hire is by building a Model" and if it's not maybe I can write a book and it will become THE business book for America and there'll be a movie and stints on national media outlets.

I say this so people know this has been a long arduous journey of fits and starts that took continuous detours until I believe I found my way to this Promise Land.

There are lots and lots and lots and loads and loads and loads of books out there about behavioral interviewing. Shoot you can pretty much find a million or so behavior-based questions on the internet. What's interesting is that for every book out there for prospective employers, for every question out there, there's a complimentary book for prospective employees, so you end up seeing titles like the following:

150 of the Best Behavior Based Interview Questions for Employers

and

150 Answers to 150 of the Best Behavior Based Interview Questions for Applicants.

Neither of the preceding titles is real that I know of, but I was struck by the similarities in titles for employers and titles for applicants. I actually have had greater success when I give the applicants my questions about five or ten minutes before the interview begins. They tend to relax, the interview becomes more of a conversation and they don't know the answer I'm looking for anyway, so I haven't found a downside. I only tell you this because almost everyone approaches the interview with an "I've got to keep this secret" mind-set and with this process with a Model that mind-set is not necessary as knowing the questions doesn't necessarily determine whether the person we're interviewing is the answer.

That's a gigantic difference between this process of building a Model and the normal interview process. I have a Model and I'm looking for someone who most closely resembles this specific Model. In the traditional interview, or even to some extent the behavioral interview, we're looking for the person who sells himself or herself to us the best.

Think about that for a moment.

Aren't we? Aren't we looking for the person that sells themselves best?

I've sat in on maybe a gazillion interviews. Maybe not that many. Maybe it's just 2,500, but there have been a lot of interviews in the last couple of decades. For a lot of them I'm just there listening to what is being asked.

I never cease to be amazed by the lack of depth of the questions some folks ask and consider legitimate. And this has nothing to do with "legal" or "illegal," which I don't really believe there are either (illegality steps in I think when we use an answer to make a determination not related to the work: "she won't fit here because…well, she's a she"). This has to do with legitimacy as it relates to someone being able to perform in the job.

"Do you like to sweat because this is a warehouse and we sweat a lot?"

"Do you like to work hard because we work hard?"

"Are you honest?"

"What would you do if someone told you to do something illegal?"

"We start work at 8:00 A.M. Can you be here by 8:00 A.M...every day?"

☆ ☆ ☆ ☆ ☆
☆ ☆ ☆ ☆ ☆
☆ ☆ ☆ ☆ ☆
☆ ☆ ☆ ☆ ☆
☆ ☆ ☆ ☆ ☆
☆ ☆ ☆ ☆ ☆
☆ ☆ ☆ ☆ ☆

The list goes on and on and on. If we're asking questions like the preceding, then is it any wonder we're hiring what we're hiring? I'll leave this conversation with the following thought:

The initial question, regardless of its quality, usually will not get us to the answer; *the next most difficult question will.*

I'll cover that, next most difficult question, concept in more depth in another chapter, but keep it in mind.

A Model is the composite of the best of the best. When we get done with it we should have a picture of the person who will perform that position as good as any person we have and possibly as good as any person can.

Let's get into our Model.

The first step is determining who are your exceptional performers in the position. I used a very clever method: I asked. I asked the supervisors across our bank's footprint who their best tellers were. And I had some supervisors who I didn't think were all that good as supervisors, or maybe they were new, or maybe I had enough names of prospective top performers, so I didn't ask everyone. I had a list of maybe 20 names. I next went to their personnel files and looked at, yes, their past performance appraisals. I looked at their raise history and I looked for any evidence contrary to their supervisor's opinion.

I tried to select as diverse a cross-section (old, young, new, tenured, male, female, Hispanic, black, white, part-time, full-time) as was possible. I didn't do this because "that's what HR does;" I did this because each demographic brings a different perspective to the equation and each brings different strengths and weaknesses. I was looking for "the composite," not "what the white people thought." When I finished this process, I took a stab and selected 8 to interview. The next four I held as my "just in case" second tier.

Then there's simply logistics of contacting each manager and explaining you've selected one of their exceptional performers. I asked the managers if I could contact the exceptional performer as I wanted a consistent message to get to these people and I never have had a lot of luck in giving a supervisor a message and having that message get through in the context I desired.

I've had too many instances where I feel like I'm a kid in grade school playing that game where you start on one side of the room with a message "Bert could be as kind as he seems" and by the time you get to the other side the message is "Part cool bees ascertain what she means."

And, most critically, most these folks were tellers, which are foundational to the success of a bank, but aren't in any significant roles in terms of "senior" management.

I was the Senior Vice President of Human Resources and Human Resources tends to freak people out and add to that "Senior Vice President" and "freak out" becomes something special in terms of

☆☆☆☆☆
☆☆☆☆☆
☆☆☆☆☆
☆☆☆☆☆
☆☆☆☆☆
☆☆☆☆☆
☆☆☆☆☆

people's reactions, so I wanted to minimize the freak out. I called these exceptional performers, explained what I was doing, set up dates and times and hit the road.

I started out with the interviewee, one-on-one, by explaining the process to her. I reiterated the reason she was chosen. "Your supervisor and I talked about it and he told me you were one of the best tellers [but could be 'whatevers'] in this business unit. I congratulate you for this, but I'd also like you to keep that between you and me as best as you can. When we build this Model we'll have something your coworkers can look at and know how they can be successful, but they won't at the moment understand what differentiates you from them. Okay? And, by helping me, you will be responsible for helping to make the company a better and more productive workplace."

I had a couple of managers who worried that "these 'exceptional' performers were going to get a big head," or that "they were going to want more money," or that "this will create discord." Usually I would respond with something like "Your concerns are very valid. Let me think about them for a bit and I'll get back with you." Then I simply never got back with them. I had plenty of managers who were more excited than the interviewee at being chosen as "one of the best." I went with them. An atmosphere that is welcoming is always easier to work in than one that is filled with trepidation, fear and nonsensical drivel—you can write that wisdom down or highlight that if you want.

What I find when identifying a super performer on the way to defining a Model is that you'll fairly quickly, in two or three interviews, find four or five or six attributes that are consistent. And I don't have a rule about the number of attributes; I'd say four to seven would seem reasonable; if you come up with less you may have these "Essential Functions," these "Critical Attributes" too broad and more than seven and you may have them too narrow, but you have to decide. And these five or six attributes will come up with almost every exceptional performer you talk with when you ask something simple of the exceptional performer or her manager like "Tell me what do you think makes you successful in your job."

When I asked this of my premier tellers every single one of them almost without hesitation said "I think it's my ability to build a relationship with my customer." The words and sentence structure were different, but the sentiment was the same.

When building a Model of a position I'd try to make these queries simple and very broad like the preceding. Then, as you need additional detail, and generally I'd wait to ask at the end of the interview, ask the specific questions. "You said that you even know things about their kids and their kids' ballgames and stuff like that; how do you go about learning that stuff?" "What made you think that information was important?" I moved from the very general to the more specific as I needed additional information. The key is to get them talking and to listen and take great notes and then at the end go back if you have to ask a specific question.

Let the interviewees, the people you're using to build your Model, guide the process. Try not to start out with specifics like "Tell me what pre-employment tests you'd recommend to test for the skills necessary to perform this job." These folks are your best performers. They're going to perform at the top of their game for you, but you can't fence them in with a bunch of little questions delving into the nitty-gritty. If you start talking about what time they come to work I'd call a "King's X, Time-Out, Do Over" and do just that: restart the thing because somewhere you got way off track. Very general to very specific (at the end of the interview, and only if need be).

And like all good interviews we should be working real hard to actively listen, take very copious notes and not talk very much. Depending on the person you're interviewing the question in the preceding may be the only one you have to ask. Try to find one or two of the most gregarious people to start with. Gregarious people are more apt to supply an abundance of information that you can then take and ask more directed questions for the folks in our midst who simply don't like to talk that much.

One of the more interesting things you'll find, I believe, is that with almost every position you're going to cover the gambit of personalities. I interviewed tellers who were jump off the page adrenaline junkies and I interviewed tellers that were almost comatose, but each and every one of them was one of our most exceptional performers. They simply got to the top using their unique personalities, an attribute of an exceptional performer.

So, if you enter this exercise thinking "well, I need a very out-going person as this position is selling," you've already set yourself up not to define what you need, but to confine yourself to what you think you need, or possibly what you have. You'll find in an array of super-

☆ ☆ ☆ ☆ ☆

☆ ☆ ☆ ☆ ☆

☆ ☆ ☆ ☆ ☆

☆ ☆ ☆ ☆ ☆

☆ ☆ ☆ ☆ ☆

☆ ☆ ☆ ☆ ☆

☆ ☆ ☆ ☆ ☆

☆ ☆ ☆ ☆ ☆

successful sales people those that get there with an overpowering personality and those that get there with quiet confidence. A trait you'll undoubtedly find, however, in a successful salesperson is persistence and persistence is not the result of volume (I'd also like to find a job description that has "persistence" listed as a key attribute).

Big CAUTION: Be careful entering this process with predetermined attributes. I made that mistake when I set out on my quest to define the ultimate high performance teller, but I had enough folks willing to tell me enough times things like "are you outta your mind?" that very quickly I quit asking about my predetermined things (except to confirm they were either important or not important, and, actually, none turned out to be important). Most folks I think will tell you if you're off in left field, if you appear to be open to receive this message, but the best way to avoid this is simply by not starting out there.

Be careful, too, bringing in old stuff to a new process and thinking you have research. A bit ago I was working with an organization. They had developed an exceptional mentoring and training program. They were hiring sales managers fresh out of college. Because this is a technology company, they were needing "technology types" (computer scientists, engineers, etc.), but because like most the rest of the world they have to sell things, they were also needing "sales personalities."

We sat down and they proudly showed me what they had done, "to date!"

They had done a lot and most of it was impressive. They had a color binder that a marketing firm had worked on and it was beautiful and catchy. They had all their materials neatly packed in this presentation binder that was pretty stunning. They had the application in the packet. About the only thing I didn't see that I probably would have recommended was they had nothing remotely related to technology in the packet. It was all paper-and-pencil. I probably would have at least included a DVD, or one of those more cool mini-DVDs cut in a unique shape or a flash drive, or checked out a little, cheap mp3 player with the company's logo on it, or something. Something. More technical.

About 18 months prior to my involvement they had already started their first class, gathering 15 recent college graduates (all male except one female, and all Caucasians, which I would have definitely changed through a stronger recruiting effort because the right diversity builds incredible strength). This first group would "graduate" in about six months, but there was a concern because the group seemed to easily grasp the technology-side of the equation and they had the management theory down pretty much to a science, but they "weren't aggressive sales guys," so I was being asked to provide them with a Model that would develop this final leg of their three-legged stool.

I asked the following question of the person, Jeff, who had proudly presented their material (and he should have been proud as it was real, real nice and expensive), "how did you go about developing your Model that you recruited from."

He looked at me blankly.

"How did you go about developing your job description?"

☆ ☆ ☆ ☆ ☆
☆ ☆ ☆ ☆ ☆
☆ ☆ ☆ ☆ ☆
☆ ☆ ☆ ☆ ☆
☆ ☆ ☆ ☆ ☆
☆ ☆ ☆ ☆ ☆
☆ ☆ ☆ ☆ ☆
☆ ☆ ☆ ☆ ☆

He stammered around for a minute and then said "I sort of stole from others and grabbed three or four job descriptions from other businesses and mashed something together and then we all [meaning the other three senior managers in the room] agreed with it and that's where it came from."

Then I asked, "Do you have anyone you know of that is doing the job you want done and doing it really well?"

"We had a guy named Ted R..., but he went to work for Dell as they were able to pay more. I hated to lose him. He could do the job of three people, but they were offering more money. He's really the reason we started this mentor program because we had no bench strength when he left. He was what we wanted to hire."

"Did you ever talk to him?"

"Talk to him?"

"Yeah, you know ask him how he does his job, what makes him tick, what's he done that worked and what he's done that doesn't work, asked him about his personality, his approach, why he did things the way he did things?"

"No, he left."

Obviously what they had done was inadvertently hired an exceptional employee, but rather than pay him what he was worth, even though he was doing the work of three people, they lost him to one of the big dogs of technology, Dell. Then, they had a really good plan, but failed to fully develop it. They weren't hiring another sales management person like what they lost in Ted; they were using job descriptions to hire what they currently had. Ted had been an accident and they couldn't replicate it with the science they were using.

Important, CRITICAL, lesson number four about Models. *Let The Model come to You.*

No preconceived notions. You're going in with a blank slate. "Must be upright and able to fog up a mirror" is probably too much preconceived notion as someone, somewhere in your interviews is going to test the first assumption in the preceding. And you may get one of those shocking moments by doing this. You may run across someone you're interviewing who presents a Model that defies logic.

Whether you agree with him and his party or not, I look at Senator Barack Obama's run for the Democratic nomination as my example of definitions in defying logic. And politics aside, one would be hard-pressed to argue that Barack Obama's campaign didn't turn some heads and change some minds about how things need to be done.

Before Obama campaigns were funded the old fashioned way: A candidate would form an exploratory committee and determine how much interest amongst her best friends there was in her running and more importantly how many different people could be pulled out of the woodwork to pump the money well. They'd have a target budget, sort of guess at what they'd need to spend for the campaign and go out and start making phone calls.

Obama and his team entered the realm with a different paradigm. They had to. Senator Clinton had the big money sewn up. Rather than look for 25 people willing to raise a $1,000,000 each, Obama's team looked for a million donors willing to invest $25 each and then they kept going back again and again and again for another $5, another $10, another $50, another $100. When all was said and done Barack Obama's campaign raised more money in the primaries alone than had ever been raised in any campaign for any office in the country and he also had a couple million people financially invested in the outcome.

Early in the campaign with Senator McCain I heard Senator McCain was off to another fundraiser. Senator Obama raised $55 million one month and never held a fundraiser. The amount of money he can raise in a single, simple, ZERO-COST, electronic request is staggering. He can come up with $30,000,000 by asking everyone for $15. The paradigm is such a dramatic shift that Clinton, arguably one of the most intelligent people in politics, and her campaign couldn't figure it out and then McCain and his campaign came up with a website and they tried to copy everything on their website to make it look and feel like Obama's, but they don't understand the people they're asking for support don't comprehend the internet in this way and only think "you mean if I go to the party I need to bring a $2,300 check and bring ten friends willing to do the same, but if I go on-line I only have to donate $25?" They're primarily business people and are doing cost/benefit analysis and have determined $25 is a lot cheaper than $2,300 and not bringing 10 friends is a lot less time consuming than bringing ten friends. The Obama paradigm doesn't even look at either of these as part of their equation.

My daughter, who worked for Obama, talks about an event that a coworker, an "older" coworker, was setting up. The coworker sent out emails to his email address book of 200 people and received a dozen or so commitments back. My daughter sent a "blast" on her Facebook the morning of the event and by that evening of the event had 130 responses. Her coworker was all nervous because she waited until the last minute; she was all "don't worry, watch what Facebook can do."

I didn't even understand Facebook at the time. I barely understood YouTube. I had heard about MySpace, which I guess had like seven users. She was using Google Docs one day and I didn't even know this powerful tool was in existence. In that technology, or possibly one that is coming, available on the web, usually for free, is a dramatic paradigm shift waiting to be discovered. It may be open for your company. We can ill afford to miss these because our minds are closed. There's someone sitting in an organization right now that could change the way the organization does business; they're using the tool right now.

There's a great little book, *Barack, Inc.* that talks about how the Obama Campaign set up his social networking campaign. To show you how powerful are these paradigm things there are people who have quit reading because I mentioned "Barack."

When I do a presentation on this stuff I invariably mention this book and the Senator's campaign a number of times. More conservative people in the audience sometimes come up afterwards and lament my advocating for "Obama." People with a more liberal slant come up to me and say things like "I thought you were a conservative?" I'm not promoting President Obama, his agenda, his ideas, or my politics. I'm saying *Barack, Inc.* is worth a read for its ideas, the book's ideas that happened to be a result of Senator Obama's campaign for the Presidency.

And Senator Bernie Sanders then took the "little donations" concept to a whole new level. I'm not sure if he read the book.

Neither of the preceding "more conservative," or "more liberal" I described just a moment ago is ready for the next paradigm shift. They're locked into that artificial definition of themselves as "Democrats" or "Republicans" and have missed the shift and will miss the future shift. I could use *The Southwest Airlines Way* as another example of a company that shifted the paradigm of an industry. Will folks in the audience who fly Continental exclusively not read this book?

Don't shoot the messenger; evaluate the message. Don't miss the paradigm shift that's coming simply because it's "Obama," or it's "McCain," it's "Romney," "Trump," "big oil" or whoever or whatever. That is silly and sad.

Listen intently, listen actively and take copious notes. One of your top performers may change your world. For example, what if one of my tellers had said "you know this brick and mortar building stuff is all good and well, but I could do everything except distribute cash out of my house and here's how we can get the cash to them...," I wonder if I would have been listening to the implications? Or if my paradigm would have kicked in and said "Oh, sure, whatever, but tell me do you generally get to work at 8 A.M?"

Think of the dramatic implications there are in your business if someone simply knows they can do their job without "flying to Singapore," or "without coming into an office," or "without the 80,000 square foot warehouse and 97 people in Toledo." And I'm not advocating that the warehouse in Toledo be closed and 97 more people be thrown out on the street by "corporate America," but I am advocating our business survive and a business' survival sometimes means the business must be redefined.

You probably won't learn these sorts of "oh my gosh" things in your interviews of your exceptional performers, but be actively listening hard enough that if someone says something you hear it and it's in your notes. Their comment may change your business model to the point that your business is no longer recognizable as what you started with.

As I approached my first interview with my first exceptional teller I was most anxious to get to the specifics of pre-employment testing. I'm always looking for that easy silver bullet that will significantly reduce the level of resources dedicated to a problem. Interviewing and hiring are labor intensive processes.

I introduced an electronic, internet-based application at the bank and that was one of my better ideas as it reduced the amount of time we were spending on processing applicants from maybe 30 or 40 minutes per applicant to essentially zero. When our bank was sold, the new ownership took us way, way backwards to paper and pencil applications and reintroduced us to a process that was mind-numbing in terms of resource allocation and we probably spent an hour to ninety minutes on each applicant again where we used to not touch the application.

At the teller line the surviving bank introduced technology so old that finding replacement parts was difficult. They literally had to go to China to find parts our industry had discarded 20 years before. This was part of the plan and they admitted their technology was from the dark ages. Their admission, although most honest, didn't make the transition backwards easier.

So, I'm a silver bullet guy. If I could determine that "10-key by touch" was the critical skill that determined whether someone was a glorious success as a teller, or whether someone was simply okay, then I could simply test for 10-key and eliminate those without the prerequisite skill. I had in my mind three areas where I could test: 10-key, computer literacy and math skills.

My reasoning was quite simple. I had watched the tellers a lot as I prepared to go out on my interviews. I had read and reread every job description I could find. The really good tellers flew on the 10-key and they used this equipment without even glancing at it ("10-key by touch"). They were on the computer, working with customers quite a bit and they counted money, so "computer skills" and "math skills" were easy to come up with. I didn't even know if I needed to ask about the math skills. They counted money. They had to know math.

☆☆☆☆☆
☆☆☆☆☆
☆☆☆☆☆
☆☆☆☆☆
☆☆☆☆☆
☆☆☆☆☆
☆☆☆☆☆

This was my paradigm and I felt it was about as accurate as any I had ever had.

I sat with my first designated great teller and asked her to talk about her job and she filled in a bunch of holes and surprised me because she talked a lot about "relationship building," like a really good bartender (I had been one of those, not "really good," but a bartender) who listens to her patrons, my teller listened, empathized and built a relationship, like a good salesperson, with her customers. I took copious notes as "relationship building" was an obvious skill set I'd want to focus more attention on in coming interviews with other exceptional tellers and it surprised me.

I was feeling pretty good about myself. I'd taken copious notes on the very first question and felt like I had uncovered one of the jewels I was looking for. And I was working hard at listening.

With my initial question I generated several pages of notes. We delved more into relationships and the attributes necessary to create this sort of environment. Not one time did any of my "hard" skills—10-key, computers, math—come up, so toward the end of the interview I began asking specifics.

"If I were looking for some pre-employment testing I could use to determine whether a teller was going to be exceptional or just okay, would you think using the 10-key without looking, by touch, would be important?"

"Well, it might be, but I didn't even know what a 10-key was when I started, so it would have excluded me."

That sort of threw me for a minute and we kind of talked about why the 10-key wasn't important to this teller, but I felt my coming interviews would confirm my paradigm and this was probably just a fluke.

"Well, you all seem to be on the computer quite a bit and so I'm assuming that having some computer skills is probably a requirement and that these skills could be tested for even before we conduct an interview."

"Oh, I don't know if they're all that important. You know the computer is like the 10-key. The first day it's pretty hard and then the second it's a bit easier and I'd say within five or six days, because we use this stuff so much, we're pretty comfortable 10-keying or using the computer, so I don't think you can really test for that, at least not to exclude someone from consideration as it just doesn't matter that much. Plus the teller platform we use on the computer isn't anything like Word or Excel, so I'm not sure there's much that relates."

Hmm. Paradigm two would need to be confirmed in later interviews. After all this interview was just the beginning. We talked some more and then just because there was this little voice in the back of my brain asking me the math question I decided to ask:

"Well, I see you all counting money a lot and so I'm wondering what sort of math test you would advocate us using as a pre-employment tool?"

"Math test?"

"Yes, you know you all have to know how to add and subtract and I would think probably divide and multiply, and I'm thinking sometimes you are dealing with some pretty big numbers and so I'm thinking you're probably functioning at the eleventh or twelfth grade level and I can test for that."

"Gosh, I guess I better pass on that one. I mean I'm just horrible at math, but the machines do all the work and then when we count the money back to the customer we put it all in the machine and the machine double-checks our work and I probably am a little better at math now because the machine catches my errors, but I'm still not very good at math."

I understood what this teller was saying about the math skills and catching errors. When I was in college I couldn't spell. I would turn in an English paper and it would get shredded in red ink and I ended up using words like "dog," "Dick" and "Jane" a lot because I knew I could spell those.

In high school where I was an equally bad speller my teachers would say, my parents would say, "well, just look the word up." I had a similar experience with an English professor who loved my writing even though she couldn't read what it was I was saying because of the spelling errors. She said "Rex, get yourself a dictionary, pre-MS Word spellcheck, and look the word up." I said "which ones?"

I think there was a realization that came over her as there was over me. I had no more idea that my spelling of "nat" was wrong and that it should be "gnat" than I had of my spelling of "that," "cat" or "Jane." They all looked right to me and the only way I could "look up the word" would be to look up every single word.

The computer and spellcheck, oh glorious spellcheck, saved me. I became a decent speller because spellcheck caught my errors.

My first interviewee became better at math because the machines looked everything up and told her she was in error. The logic of this process is almost the exact opposite of how most of us think: we shouldn't have focused on "math skills;" the focus should have been on "follow the process."

I had four more interviews that afternoon, but I cancelled them. I went back to my office and thought about this initial interview. A lot. It had knocked me off stride. I slowly began to realize that I had conducted this interview not to root out the core competencies of an exceptional performer, but to confirm my paradigm. And my paradigm, what I viewed a successful teller as, and what reality was, were far, far apart.

This may seem a bit melodramatic, but that is not my intent. My goal in this process I thought was to build a Model of what the best teller in our world looked like. Then we could simply hire to that Model. As it turned out because of the power of my paradigm I was only pretending to investigate. My goal had actually been to confirm my paradigm. Erase, erase, erase. King's X, time-out, do over.

Still, in the back of my mind, there was that little voice saying "she's only one teller, Rex. She's only one. The others will tell you it's 10-key by touch, computer literacy and most importantly math skills."

But the others did not.

Actually, they…all of them…confirmed the exact opposite and reinforced my first interview.

The consistency of what they said and what their managers affirmed was truly a remarkable outcome. When I completed the process I had no doubt I had defined our Model and I had no doubt that if I could get our managers to change their paradigm I could bring about a revolutionary change in our bank. I had built an exceptional process, my Model.

The "revolutionary change," I thought, was a bit of a stretch, but it was not. To this day I still work on creating that change, but my Model is a flawless concept—it's the science of hiring I had been seeking for years and years. I had found my Holy Grail.

Chapter 6
Selecting
The Ring

The only way to build a Model is to start. Like we've discussed, (1) find the absolute best performers in a specific role that you can (according to any objective measures you have and according to supervisors' opinions), (2) start with broad, open-ended questions working to the specific and (3) take some fairly copious notes, but at the right time.

That's about it. I start my interviews the following (after I first tell them I'm not there because anyone is in trouble—so stellar was the reputation of the head of HR that I first had to dispel this belief and even then I had to constantly reinforce it) way: "Your supervisor speaks very highly of your performance and I congratulate you for your effort. I'm here to try to define what it is you do differently than even perhaps your coworkers that makes your supervisor so high on you. In that vein please describe for me your day and your interactions with customers and anything you might see, or think, you do differently."

A quick note, too. You might also look at someone who has recently promoted (within the last 3 months) from a "lower-level" position to a higher level position. Like, for example, when I interviewed Tellers I was looking at Tellers of course, but I was also looking at the next level above (Senior Tellers, or Customer Service Managers, or Banking Assistants). If a Customer Service Manager had recently been a Teller and had been promoted, the chances are he or she was doing an outstanding job as a Teller. I didn't just select these folks because they'd been promoted, but if all the "this is a superstar" criteria aligned, he or she was part of my pool.

That's really usually all I need to ask and then I get real quiet. I'm not looking either for *War and Peace: The Sequel*. I'm looking for perhaps one or two pages of type written notes. Remember, we're only looking to define the three or four of five critical things this person does that others may not, or more than likely don't do as well. And my later interviews will probably be shorter than my first interviews because I begin looking for confirming data and looking less at something new that suddenly "pops up."

If I'm on my seventh interview (which, I would think you could get by with three to five), and all of a sudden this seventh Teller says "and I like to give the customer a little something, a pen, a sticky note pad, to insure he comes back" I'm not going to go back and ask the other Tellers if they do this too. If the attribute isn't in the clear majority, then it may get honorable mention, but it may also get ignored.

And I want to delve deeply into this Model I built for my Teller position so that you have a structure and a model that you can use when starting work on yours. The following sentence will make you want to either pass out or have a cow, so please read it and then let me explain it. My 3-ring binder, that I used for training was 186 pages long.

☆ ☆ ☆ ☆ ☆
☆ ☆ ☆ ☆ ☆
☆ ☆ ☆ ☆ ☆
☆ ☆ ☆ ☆ ☆
☆ ☆ ☆ ☆ ☆
☆ ☆ ☆ ☆ ☆
☆ ☆ ☆ ☆ ☆

Yours could be seven or eight pages, but definitely under 10. Let me explain the difference.

My Teller Model was the full "how to." In essence, this work you're reading in a 3-ring binder, less all the clever witticisms, but with much greater detail of things like behavior-based interview questions and the structure of those questions. Printed, the PowerPoint presentation was 29 pages. That wasn't all slides that were displayed as I'm not a big believer in boring people into a coma with PowerPoint, but I'm also a big proponent of training people will actually be more likely to look at and possibly use, so I interspersed the presentation slides with quotes that seemed relevant like "Winning is not a sometime thing; it's an all time thing. You don't win once in a while, you don't do things right once in a while, you do them right all the time. Winning is habit. Unfortunately, so is losing."

That one comes from Vince Lombardi, former coach of the world champion Green Bay Packers football team. I included it in my presentation manual for ulterior motives. Lombardi is also credited with having said "Winning isn't everything. It's the only thing." However, if you think about that quote for a minute, it's not something a coach would say. What that preceding line says if you don't win, you're a loser. Although the Packers were good, they weren't always good and even when they were things happened and they would lose a game here and there. A coach won't call his or her team losers.

What Lombardi apparently actually said was "Winning isn't everything, but making the effort to win is." Somewhere the core meaning got lost in someone's translation and admittedly the one most of us remember is catchier; it's simply less what a coach would say.

I don't have a spectacular reason for telling you this. I'm always interested in listening to what people say. I never liked the quote ascribed to Lombardi. It didn't seem like something a great coach would say: "Win or you're a bunch of losers" and, so, any chance I get I propose the other quote. Both are taken from people's memories so neither may be right.

So, 29 of my pages were filled with PowerPoint and quotes. Then I read a bunch of books in preparation for defining my Model. I wanted to see what other authors were saying about hiring and getting good talent. I took each of these and I typed out all the passages I had highlighted as I read. When I gave these to managers, I went a step further and highlighted the critical pieces of information from my highlights. Therefore, a manager could turn to *The Talent Edge* by David S. Cohen. There were 24 pages of my notes from *The Talent Edge*. There were probably one or two pages of highlighted passages. *Interviewing and Selecting High Performers* by Richard h. Beatty was 7 pages of notes. *Interviewing: More Than a Gut Feeling* by Richard S. Deems was also 7 pages. *The Southwest Airlines Way* by Jody Hoffer Gittell was 17 pages and was probably the most enjoyable to read and Southwest is a great model to use for this stuff. And so it went for another 10 or 15 pages.

I did the preceding for a number of reasons. First, I needed my managers to accept my direction as expert opinion. By showing them I was gleaning information from experts they were more inclined to think of my opinions in this regard. Second, I didn't know everything and still don't. Others have great information and I wanted to show my managers that there was other great stuff out there. Third, and finally, I like to read and I like to give others the benefit of what I'm reading and most won't take the time, so hopefully a few folks that went through my training read some of my notes and perhaps even picked up a book or two.

Then I had a spirally bound insert titled "Defining the Superstar CSR (Customer Service Representative [CSR] was how we referred to our Tellers—the re-titling of a Teller to CSR never took, but the idea was a good one and if we had more "Superstars," they would have probably all thought of themselves as CSRs). This spiral-bound piece was 63 pages long. I not only gave all the behavior-based questions to use I also gave some possible answers and what to look for.

Back matter to the binder, which included a few notes on interviewing, advertisements for newspapers, and a printout of an Excel spreadsheet I had developed. The Excel spreadsheets allowed managers to go through and pick 10 or 15 questions and then the spreadsheet automatically built the questionnaire. The final few pages were an example of the questionnaire.

The depth of this exercise is far more involved than yours needs to be. If you want someone to train this magnificent Model building with your managers or HR folks, you might consider contacting me (rcastle263@gmail.com; no, I'm anything but free, but I'm going to save you a fortune—I'll guarantee you that).

If you want to define a Model yourself, then simply use what you're currently reading. I wanted my managers to begin at least thinking about defining Models for themselves. Easily our highest turnover was in Tellers and I didn't have the time to define every position in the company. Our managers were doing the hiring; they needed the understanding of the skill sets to define their own Models.

Let's delve into this Model.

I believe what most of you will put together is a one or two page Model that gives a very good snapshot of the composite "perfect" person in a particular position. Here's what a similar snapshot of my Superstar Teller looked like.

"Our Superstar CSR is first and foremost a customer service junky and a relationship building guru. These two traits came out over and over and over. In almost every answer customers were talked about. Even when I asked them about the equipment that was most important to doing their job: 'The computer because it speeds up transactions for our customers.' Training? 'I like training that lets me serve my customers better.' 'Customer service' was the focus. We can use this when we're selecting someone because we should get a real good sense of whether they believe in providing exceptional customer service.

Our Superstar Teller doesn't just like people, he or she loves them. Loves being around them, loves their problems and really focuses on his or her customers' and coworkers' relationships from this angle. We can use this in our interviews even at the point when we're doing interviews as we should be able to start analyzing how this potential Teller works around people.

Our Superstar Teller is almost always in a good mood (at work and he or she makes a conscious decision to be in this mood), is more often than not smiling and will apologize to a customer at the drop of a hat regardless of who is 'right' or who is 'wrong.' We can use this during our interviews just by watching body language. Does our candidate smile easily? Are his or her eyes alive with energy? Do they seem happy?

What our Superstar Teller may or may not be is experienced, although 'money handling skills' seemed somewhat important to probably 70% or 80% of the Tellers I spoke with. What our Superstar Teller may or may not be is gregarious and outgoing. Although the one incredibly shy person I interviewed did say he or she was 'working myself out of that because you just have to around here' (this person's manager is real outgoing). What our Superstar Teller may or may not be is good with the computer, good with the 10-key, good with any of the equipment or even particularly good with math (although cash handling skills were seen as important). We can use all of this to realize that these things are really second-tier considerations. Look for customer service, relationship building, team players and then if you have to separate one from the other, use the harder skills—according to the Superstar Tellers doing the jobs, these things (outside of money handling experience) simply were not and are not important to their success.

In a nutshell, the preceding is a composite sketch of our Superstar Teller (and of course there are variations, so if you know one of the

☆ ☆ ☆ ☆ ☆ _____
☆ ☆ ☆ ☆ ☆ _____
☆ ☆ ☆ ☆ ☆ _____
☆ ☆ ☆ ☆ ☆ _____
☆ ☆ ☆ ☆ ☆ _____
☆ ☆ ☆ ☆ ☆ _____
☆ ☆ ☆ ☆ ☆ _____
☆ ☆ ☆ ☆ ☆ _____

folks I interviewed and they're not in a good mood most the time, view this trait in them as the exception and not the norm)."

The preceding is "my Model." The questions that follow are directed at fleshing out whether someone has the attributes described in the preceding. Your Models will appear similar to the preceding. The attributes may or may not change. A "Computer Programmer" would probably think computer literacy important (probably). The object of a Model is to finish with an accurate picture of what the composite of your best performers look like.

You use behavior-based questions, then, to see if your candidate aligns to your Model. This is radically different than using behavior-based questions to see if a candidate has the attributes listed in a job description. And with that said now you should be able to see very clearly the difference between the preceding narrative and a job description. Following is a list of tasks from a traditional Teller's job description:

- Primary function is performing various paying and receiving Teller activities while providing excellent customer service with minimal balancing errors.
- Knowledgeable of the services and products offered by the Bank.
- Provide customer service in a friendly, courteous and professional manner and represent the Bank, with a positive attitude.
- Knowledge of standard office equipment such as duplicating machines, telefax, laser printers, PC, and related software,

☆☆☆☆☆
☆☆☆☆☆
☆☆☆☆☆
☆☆☆☆☆
☆☆☆☆☆
☆☆☆☆☆
☆☆☆☆☆

- such as Word for Windows, Excel and other EDS software or specialized accounting software.
- Must be well organized and able to set priorities.
- Able to perform under pressure and effectively work at problem solving.
- Makes decisions and utilizes resources to accomplish goals and maintain confidentiality of personnel and other sensitive bank matters.
- Skilled at verbal and written communication as well as effective listening and interpersonal skills.

The Model is a narrative that draws a picture of the person we are looking for; the job description is a list of tasks.

And a bunch of the following is taken from narrative I developed for several models of Tellers for different entities. I didn't change a lot of the wording to make it "more generic." Copying the following work is simply a matter of inserting the job title you're modeling and defining your culture. The following should give you a real, real good idea of the variables associated with a Model, a real, real good template to use to develop your own.

One of the features that will stand out in any organization, and therefore needs some attention, is the organization's culture. If you're culture is casual and somewhat laid back, be careful hiring a fire-breathing, take-no-prisoner salesperson. Usually the opposite happens. We're looking for someone to set the world on fire and we get a wet blanket.

☆☆☆☆☆
☆☆☆☆☆
☆☆☆☆☆
☆☆☆☆☆
☆☆☆☆☆
☆☆☆☆☆
☆☆☆☆☆
☆☆☆☆☆

By way of example, let me incorporate some of what I learned about the bank's culture and how I married it to the interview and selection process because we can hire the best of the best of the best, but if they fail to fit into our culture, they're probably not going to succeed. Therefore you need to figure out what it is your company values and what your culture looks like.

This can seem like a daunting task, but take a stab at it and then ask a couple of the more senior managers who have been around for a while and then ask the owner or CEO.

What I found in talking with the preceding people at the bank and also confirmed, more or less, with the Teller interviews was the bank had the following cultural attributes and values:

- Customer Service
- Employees (and teambuilding)
- Community (and community banking)
- Return to Shareholder

Once you have the culture down, you can set about the task of defining questions (which admittedly, where "Culture" is concerned, are tough) that you might be able to ask a prospective candidate.

How important is this "culture junk?"

Critically. Much turnover is driven simply because people do not fit in the culture in which they were hired. Someone who does not have a culture/values fit, therefore, should probably not be considered a viable candidate. He or she simply cannot succeed. Try mixing oil and water for a visual example.

And when you define the culture do not think of your list as exhaustive. If there are multiple locations, especially if they're located in more diverse geographies, you may find they value other things. However, the preceding four I found were the ones senior management believed were critical values of our company and this group is in the leadership position and where a definition of culture is concerned their opinion must carry significant weight. As I mentioned, too, you will also confirm, with the possible exception of "Return to Shareholders" with one-on-one interviews with your candidates. Tell your managers, they can add additional values, but the preceding four (and yours will be dependent on your company and maybe more or less than four—one or two is probably too few; six or seven maybe too many) are the core and should be part of any interview when attempting to determine whether a candidate "fits our culture."

You'll see geographic differences. I found two in developing the preceding model for this bank for this position: (1) West Texas (excluding El Paso) and New Mexico and (2) El Paso.

El Paso seemed to have more of a "big bank" mentality, while the other Tellers from other locations seemed to embrace the idea of "community." El Paso people, too, tended to focus more on the "rules" and "doing things right." Other Tellers from other locations were more focused on "relationship building." Neither of these possibly perceived dichotomies was more "right" than the other. The smaller areas tend to focus on the attributes of a "rural" community; one of these is smallness and the associated relationship building. El Paso is a lot of things; small is probably not one of these. With larger groups a more "controlled" environment is often seen and therefore a heavier reliance on "the rules."

And sometimes you're going to run across some seeming conflicts. There was one I hit when I was looking at El Paso Tellers as they were very "rule" dominant. Others never mentioned "rules," but the folks from El Paso had this as a major talking point. Pulling together a composite, therefore, can be a bit challenging.

However, overwhelmingly the "rule followers" were in a very small minority to the "relationship builders" and even the "rule followers" spoke of "relationship building" and "customer service" as the number one aspects, the foundations, of their job. The split came when I went below the first level of task importance. Then, we saw some divergence in terms of what the various Tellers thought to be important about doing a "superstar" job. You'll undoubtedly run across similar seemingly polar opposites. You're building a composite and you'll have to work toward what is most prevalent (not compromise) and use your best judgment without prejudice (pre-judgment).

Then, you're going to have to come up with some ways to evaluate the "cultural fit" of a candidate. I didn't think what I did in this first Model was particularly good. At the same time when you go from asking nothing about culture to listening and watching for clues and trying to ask questions to get to a cultural fit, you have to think you'll be doing a far cry better than nothing. What you're trying to do is insure a cultural match. Without this match you're probably not going to have a long-term relationship as the person you hire will feel like the proverbial fish out of water.

Also most of the time, your queries are going to be exploring several attributes at once. And that's okay. We're not animals that think in terms of one thing or one area. Usually our brain ranges around the gambit and then may come back with "Did I answer your question?" Many times there is too much overlap. I'm going to give a few example questions in the following, but I'm not suggesting you'd go into an interview and ask them in succession. The first may yield the exact same answer as the second. By the time you get to the third, the interviewee might be simply saying "what I said on number one." Another hurdle to keep in mind is exploring "cultural fit" from a behavior-based standpoint can be very difficult and fairly useful information can be gleaned from the application (looking at the candidate's past positions and employers) and when checking references asking questions specific to culture and not currently part of anyone's "form." I almost guarantee it. Finally "Customer service," a part of the preceding list of core values is not specifically covered in the following queries as this is a major aspect of the Teller's role and this value is explored later under the competency queries.

Here are some stabs, however, at trying to get at the culture beast (query, followed by things to look for in the answer):

Tell us about the companies you've worked for in the past and what you believe these companies valued and why?

☆ ☆ ☆ ☆ ☆
☆ ☆ ☆ ☆ ☆
☆ ☆ ☆ ☆ ☆
☆ ☆ ☆ ☆ ☆
☆ ☆ ☆ ☆ ☆
☆ ☆ ☆ ☆ ☆
☆ ☆ ☆ ☆ ☆
☆ ☆ ☆ ☆ ☆

Answer: Pretty straightforward in terms of what you are looking for in a response. If your candidate happens to mention customer service, now would be a perfect time to ask a follow-up: "When you say 'customer service' please give us a specific example from your past that might show us what you mean when you use this term." "Return to Shareholders" may never come up, especially for folks who have never worked, or worked at a fast food restaurant or some other similar endeavor. Anything where the word "profit" is thrown around is probably a conversation worth exploring. A candidate might say something like the following: "Our company was always talking about making a profit; this was real important to them and we all sort of developed this way of thinking. Because making money is always going to be the goal of a company." Cities and government entities probably would be looking for things related to maximizing the taxpayers' dollar, but the concept is essentially the same. As you get more comfortable with behavioral selection, you'll know not to over-acknowledge the "correctness" of an answer. "And what did that word 'profit' mean to you?" would be a good follow-up in terms of "Return to Shareholder." What you're exploring is their general understanding that we work not just so we can make a living, but so the entity we work with is viable. And someone who has no idea, or doesn't mention profit or shareholder value or any of the other ways we use to say "make money," doesn't exclude himself or herself. The understanding that the bank was interested in making a profit is not critical to our Superstar Tellers' ability to perform at the outset of their employment, but probably is critical as they look to continue their careers and possibly get into management. You may not want to hire someone who thinks of a for-profit entity, like a bank, in a not-for-profit sense— and this may come up, but rarely.

☆☆☆☆☆
☆☆☆☆☆
☆☆☆☆☆
☆☆☆☆☆
☆☆☆☆☆
☆☆☆☆☆
☆☆☆☆☆

Tell us if the companies you have worked with in the past were involved in the communities where you worked, and, if they were, how were they involved and, if they weren't, why do you think this is.

Answer: Again, a pretty straightforward question. This analysis was for a community bank. As such they tried to be involved in their community as good corporate citizens, but also as good employee community citizens. The more involved their employees were in their communities (within reason) the better (probably).

At your past employers, describe for us the environments you worked in and the employee groups you worked with.

Answer: A good follow-up will probably be, "were these the sorts of jobs that required a lot of independence (working basically by yourself), or required a lot of interdependence (more or less relying on others)?" You'll notice I did not use the term "teamwork" in the preceding and I would advocate not using it. Who isn't for "teamwork?" If you use this word we give the candidate the answer we're seeking. The preceding is framed a little in the negative probably. Most people think "independence" is a worthwhile objective; in point of fact, however, the majority of us rely on others every day and actually tend to rely on others to adequately perform our functions—interdependence.

"Culture" is a dynamic piece of hiring the right person. Even if all the other pieces line up in your Model, a disconnect on culture is most probably a fatal flaw. And this flaw is not the fault of the candidate, or your company, or your analysis—it simply is. Please don't ignore it.

☆ ☆ ☆ ☆ ☆
☆ ☆ ☆ ☆ ☆
☆ ☆ ☆ ☆ ☆
☆ ☆ ☆ ☆ ☆
☆ ☆ ☆ ☆ ☆
☆ ☆ ☆ ☆ ☆
☆ ☆ ☆ ☆ ☆
☆ ☆ ☆ ☆ ☆

I want to take the sections of this Model I defined for Teller and lay them out here in all their detail. I want to do this because I am not sure how much information each of you will need to complete your Model and I don't want to short-sheet anyone.

If you feel as though you have enough information, your Model awaits, or you may want to take a few minutes and read through the first couple of the following and then jump on out there and start modeling, or you may be the type of person who wants to read every word to the end. Whatever your preference is of course fine; I simply wanted to let you know what was coming and why.

My composite, my Model, (that thing you read a few pages ago) consisted of someone with the following attributes:

- Relationship Building Skills
- Customer Service Skills
- People Skills (really more the ability to love people)
- Problem Solving Skills
- Ability to Follow Rules and or Procedures.

Then, there was another set of attributes that played a part in the success of the Tellers I interviewed. These attributes/behaviors included the following:

- Great attitude
- Smile a lot
- Honest

☆☆☆☆☆ _____
☆☆☆☆☆ _____
☆☆☆☆☆ _____
☆☆☆☆☆ _____
☆☆☆☆☆ _____
☆☆☆☆☆ _____
☆☆☆☆☆ _____

- Not afraid to apologize
- Likes to learn
- Knowledge of products, services, policies and procedures

I didn't really define queries for these "other attributes." I'll discuss them a little at the end, but several of them should become readily apparent in an interview and some (like "Honest") may not be easily discerned in an interview setting, which is sort of a situation where one person comes in and sells themselves (sometimes dishonestly) to another.

Outside of asking questions like "Describe for us a situation you were in where you smiled a lot," there seems to be limited ability to "test" for these behaviors. As mentioned, the interview itself is a great place to analyze most these behaviors. The final bullet point "knowledge of products, services, policies and procedures" should be viewed as an attribute that can be gleaned rather quickly by a newly hired employee. Exceptional Tellers, and all other positions I've ever analyzed, use a variety of self-initiated methods to learn a company's products and are anxious to learn about policies and the various procedures that impact their areas. I would be surprised if other "Superstars" in other industries, across other job titles did not share these desires. All the Tellers I interviewed, however, stated that this final attribute, "product knowledge," was not one we should focus on when considering who to hire as a Teller; I would test for this same conclusion during your interviews as I believe it will show validity across the spectrum.

Let me digress for a moment. And, yes, I have mentioned the following before, but the disconnect was so great it deserves the additional

☆ ☆ ☆ ☆ ☆
☆ ☆ ☆ ☆ ☆
☆ ☆ ☆ ☆ ☆
☆ ☆ ☆ ☆ ☆
☆ ☆ ☆ ☆ ☆
☆ ☆ ☆ ☆ ☆
☆ ☆ ☆ ☆ ☆
☆ ☆ ☆ ☆ ☆

space. What is most curious about the two preceding lists are some of the areas I thought were important, but were not only not mentioned by the Tellers I interviewed, but were thought to be somewhat unimportant. When I brought up "math skills" for example, the Teller would invariably say something like "okay, they're important I guess, but I really didn't have them when I came to work here; customer service is really the key." As one person I interviewed stated "You can learn how to do the ten-key, but never learn how to get a personality."

This theme is also echoed by the hiring strategy of Southwest Airlines: "hire for attitude and train for skill." Even when they're looking at a pilot, they obviously want some extraordinary skill sets and talents, but they're not looking at hiring competence to the exclusion of attitude.

And, the bank's process was focused in almost all areas on the "hard" skills. This, too, I confirmed with existing employees and how they were interviewed and the questions they were asked: "Can you add and subtract to X digits?" "Are you computer literate?" "Can you use the 10-key?" "By touch?" "How many years of 'Teller' experience do you possess?"

Companies cannot hire really happy incompetents and expect the results we need, but we should seek out folks who have the core skills and talents this process will discover and then build in areas where they may be lacking. What exceptional Tellers told me, almost to a person, was that the "hard skills" don't matter that much; the skill sets defined in my interviews, however, are the foundations on which our exceptional Tellers built their success.

☆☆☆☆☆
☆☆☆☆☆
☆☆☆☆☆
☆☆☆☆☆
☆☆☆☆☆
☆☆☆☆☆
☆☆☆☆☆

Your foundations, for the critical positions you have at your company, in your city or county, will be built in the same way.

The remainder of this chapter talks in more depth about each of the aforementioned areas that represent the composite of my exceptional Teller and offers behavior-based questions that will begin to explore each aspect of this success model. You may find this discussion very useful because many of the queries can probably be used for other job titles and industries and you'll get the rhythm, the art and the skill of the behavioral interview question. In the following I take each attribute I discovered for this Teller position in order.

Relationship Building Skills

The one aspect of a super-successful Teller that stood out above all the others, and was universal, was the Teller's ability to form relationships with his or her customers, coworkers and supervisors. What is real interesting, and something not a lot of mangers get, I believe erroneously concluding this is "soft" information that doesn't drive ROI, is the fact that extraordinarily successful companies like Southwest Airlines focus on an applicant's and employee's ability to form relationships in the company's recruiting and hiring.

How do we test for this attribute? What sorts of questions might be appropriate? We can ask both positive and negative questions to ferret out answers. However, no question will provide the answer unto itself. What we have to constantly do is seek very specific examples from a candidate's past (work or personal) that will demonstrate the traits we are looking for (or demonstrate the fact they do not possess the traits). Very specific.

Therefore, we must sometimes not be satisfied with the response the person gives us and must ask a follow-up question (or questions) until we have the answer we seek. If you find at the end of the interview that you have a series of statements that do not give you the specific information necessary to draw an informed conclusion, the chances are you needed to ask some additional, clarifying (usually tougher and less comfortable) questions. And, there may be occasions, especially as you get comfortable with this methodology, you have to schedule second interviews.

There is also no way to anticipate what these follow-up questions might consist of and therefore I may make some suggestions, but out of context I simply have a limited ability to guess at what is needed. The old adage "practice makes perfect" probably fits well here.

Not all questions, too, will be right on point. We cannot simply come out and say "do you play well with others?" We have to pick from their responses an answer to our question "how closely does this person seem to match up to our model?"

And, you don't use all the questions. Generally, you use the same questions for each interview, but don't just put all the following questions on a sheet of paper and think "these are pretty good." Your interview probably will consist of 10 to 15 queries (and then there'll be multiple follow-up questions I of course cannot anticipate).

☆☆☆☆☆ _____
☆☆☆☆☆ _____
☆☆☆☆☆ _____
☆☆☆☆☆ _____
☆☆☆☆☆ _____
☆☆☆☆☆ _____
☆☆☆☆☆ _____

Finally, some questions work and some do not. If you find a question that is not working for a particular hiring exercise, modify it, replace it or remove it. You should try to ask the same initial questions of all candidates, but don't keep using questions that multiple candidates are struggling with. This advice tends to drive an attorney bonkers, but you can modify "stupid" anytime you want without consequence. Just don't go exclude someone from an earlier interview because "she gave a really poor answer" on the question you threw out for everyone else—throw them all out and throw out all the previous responses as well.

Some of the following questions, too, are not strictly behavioral-based. Some require more work to get to these sorts of answers. Simply try to keep in mind "the best predictor of future behavior is past behavior" and you'll have a firm understanding of what we're trying to achieve with the behavior-based part of this process.

The following questions, therefore, should not be seen as an end of the process, but a good first step for comparing your stack of applicants against your Model you've built.

When we speak with three or four of your close work associates and we ask them to describe your relationships with them, what are they going to tell us?

Answer: Why use "when" when the chances are we cannot talk to three or four of their close work associates? Because the hint of this possibility increases the likelihood of a more honest response. Having someone keying in their responses on a computer for some bizarre reason also increases this "honesty" likelihood, but I wouldn't advocate this approach. As they think about this response, or immediately prior to finishing it, you might also consider passing the candidate a piece of paper and pen and telling them that you'd like them to give you a few names of people they've worked with in the past. People, of course, tend to paint the picture they want us to see and they usually don't want to paint a negative picture. By suggesting "we're going to check" the candidate has to assume we are and therefore he or she is more likely to paint a more realistic portrait. The answer to this and the next query is probably fairly self-explanatory and not necessarily behavioral-based, but still you can use follow-ups to garner more and more specific information. Be looking for someone who uses terms not necessarily associated with work. What I mean here are the "canned" responses things like "hard worker," "enjoys a challenge." But more revealing answers may be "great team player," "love to be around her or him," "super problem solver."

When we ask your most current manager to talk with us about the relationships you have with your coworkers and/or customers, what will he or she say?

Answer: Looking for the same sort of responses as in the preceding. Probably a vastly different perspective, though.

When we ask your most current manager to describe some of the instances where you have had difficulty with a relationship, what will he or she say?

☆☆☆☆☆
☆☆☆☆☆
☆☆☆☆☆
☆☆☆☆☆
☆☆☆☆☆
☆☆☆☆☆
☆☆☆☆☆

Answer: Sometimes asking for negative information is a good way to tell if (1) someone is honest (everyone always has something negative in their work life) and (2) they still demonstrate the qualities we're looking for even in negative situations. Also, you might consider asking the first question and then this one. A good follow-up to this one after their answer might be "And, the people you were talking about in your first answer, what would they say about this description of your associations at work."

Which of your personal traits have been most helpful in your ability to build relationships and why?

Answer: Few people will not realize this question is asking them to define their relationship building skills and fewer will give us negative answers for these sorts of queries and they can pretty much make stuff up about themselves, which can be verified during reference checks by simply asking the candidate's references what personal traits our candidate has that has helped him or her (the candidate) build relationships. However, things like "people say I'm friendly," "I like people," "I enjoy working with people" and other statements that point to "relationship building" are what we're looking for and, again, we're looking for things we can verify with reference checking. Again, don't accept them at face value, but you might get some useful tidbits in this line of questioning and you can follow-up with something like "You say people say you're friendly. Can you share with us a specific example of someone who might say this and why?"

What key factors have accounted for your career success and why?

☆ ☆ ☆ ☆ ☆
☆ ☆ ☆ ☆ ☆
☆ ☆ ☆ ☆ ☆
☆ ☆ ☆ ☆ ☆
☆ ☆ ☆ ☆ ☆
☆ ☆ ☆ ☆ ☆
☆ ☆ ☆ ☆ ☆
☆ ☆ ☆ ☆ ☆

Answer: See the answer to the preceding query and you'll get a pretty good idea of the types of things you're looking for.

Tell us about the best working relationship you have developed with a coworker and generally how you go about developing relationships.

Answer: This and the remaining queries are behavioral in nature. They ask for a specific instance, a specific example. By asking for "the best" you are looking at the picture of "it doesn't get any better than this" and you can then back into whether this person has the capacity to build solid relationships. Good relationship builders build long-term relationships. They hate leaving the place where they are working not because of the work, but because of the "friends" they're leaving behind. They hate leaving customers. These folks are all friends. Listen for this type of language. If the answer the candidate gives seems too far "over the top" in terms of you think you may be looking at a saint, ask the next most difficult question, "You talk about something approaching 'wonderful,' so my next obvious question is why leave?" If the person is leaving for pay, well, that's often times a reason, but all things being equal, the pay difference should be fairly substantial (as defined by them [i.e., someone making $9.75 an hour might think $10.25 is substantial; someone making $64,500 a year might not think a lot of an extra $1,000 a year.])

Describe for us a specific work relationship that you've had difficulty with and how you handled this difficulty.

Answer: Negative questions force the candidate to talk about how they behaved in a less than desirable circumstance. Some may be

☆☆☆☆☆
☆☆☆☆☆
☆☆☆☆☆
☆☆☆☆☆
☆☆☆☆☆
☆☆☆☆☆
☆☆☆☆☆

hesitant to share with you and you may have to wait several seconds and then say something like "You know we've all had things go south with this person or that person for a variety of reasons; well just the other day…" And then allow them more time to think of an answer. Someone who really "can't think of a thing" has either had limited experiences or isn't being as honest as you need. Some people, too, will share some real interesting information. Watch for folks I call "cauldron stirrers." These immature (not young, but immature) people are the ones who keep the workplace in absolute turmoil by gossiping, backbiting, favoritism and never accepting responsibility for any failure in a relationship. They also will talk about these experiences from the standpoint of "I was right" and therefore identifying them is often not difficult. Don't accept non-specific responses: "I've known some people who seemed kind of hostile." Your response would be "Good, let's talk about one of these people as a specific example and you don't have to use their name, but tell me exactly what happened between the two of you." Note the "between the two of you." You don't care if the person you're talking to is the consummate referee. You want to know about their behavior. Oh, and I'd advocate not hiring a referee as this "occupation" can be very time consuming and unless the referee can change things, completely counterproductive.

Tell us the methods you use to form relationships and please be as specific as possible. (NOTE: This may prove a very difficult question and the answers may be a little suspect.)

Answer: This question should yield a story and not a scientific discourse of relationship dynamics. If you get a theoretical answer, ask another question, "Well, that's a good sort of theoretical look, but now what I need for you to do is to share with me a very specific example where you show me the steps you take in building a relationship." Good relationship builders like listening to other people's "stories." They ask questions about others. They don't talk as much about "self." They demonstrate empathy [identification with and understanding of another's situation, feelings and motives]. They are focused on others not themselves. When you're listening to this answer be looking for these sorts of attributes, but also be looking for the opposites.

Describe for us a specific instance with a customer where the customer was upset and explain how you handled this difficult customer. (NOTE: Someone fresh out of high school, where this is his or her first job, will have no idea what you are asking. You might be able to reframe it to their circumstance and ask for a situation where a teacher wasn't very happy with him or her, or this question may simply be irrelevant for some.)

Answer: What you're looking for is someone with the capacity to maintain a relationship even when emotions are running hot. You'll notice later, if you read this whole work, exceptional customer-facing people, like Tellers, have a great capacity to empathize and apologize. They tend to do this to separate the problem from the customer and get on the customer's side to "fix the problem" and not "affix the blame." What you're looking for is someone with this capacity to diffuse difficult situations. I haven't asked this query of Teller candidates, but have been amazed at the responses I've received from people interviewing to work with me in human resources. Upset customers can be difficult, but a skilled and empathetic listener can bring the customer back into our court. When was the last time you

☆☆☆☆☆
☆☆☆☆☆
☆☆☆☆☆
☆☆☆☆☆
☆☆☆☆☆
☆☆☆☆☆
☆☆☆☆☆

remained angry at someone who was on your side? Listen for someone who listens, empathizes (which is different than sympathizes—one says "oh, sorry" [sympathy]; the other says "oh, do I understand where you're coming from" [empathy]).

Tell us about a time when you were involved in a difficult situation with a person and had to address that situation one-on-one with that person.

Answer: If you have a couple of just out of high school kids you're interviewing, this question may be a better one to ask than the ones regarding customers as they're probably going to have a limited understanding about what a customer is, except, of course, for those who have taken a business class and heard the teacher harp on "customer service." Then they're going to say things like "well, the customer is number one." You can avoid listening to this stuff and get into the meat of our needs by asking the preceding question of these candidates. Look for the person who is able to call a "King's X, time-out," if we're talking in kindergarten language. These folks are able to really step back from a situation, defuse the emotion and work with customers and others to attack a problem. Watch for someone who is a little too "snappish" when pushed. You should see some instances of this throughout the interview.

When was the last time you lost your temper or became upset with someone at work and how was it resolved.

Answer: People are going to be real hesitant to tell you they ever lose their temper, but all of us have muttered to ourselves "I'm so mad at my mother," or other similar things. We all do it. The question then becomes "how do we get over it." The object is not to find "the perfect person" as this person doesn't exist. The object is to find someone who solves the problem whatever it is with a smile on their face and in their voice. Please beware the person who is still upset over the split milk from several years ago. These folks have long memories and usually a capacity for using them negatively in our workplace.

Tell me about a couple of your previous supervisors and what you enjoyed about working with them.

Answer: If the candidate describes his or her wonderful supervisor and you ain't it, then you may want to consider looking at another candidate. You know better than anyone what your core is. Don't hire someone who is contrary to your core.

The most important relationship an employee can have, and this has been borne out over and over again in my interviews with stellar performers, is the one with his or her immediate supervisor. Don't hesitate to exclude someone who is looking for someone other than who you are.

Opposites attract but only if they're magnets. In relationships, opposites really don't do that well. The saying should be "People with interesting and divergent interests can be attracted to one another," but that isn't as clever or succinct as "Opposites attract." Of course my saying is true, which makes it somewhat better in some situations, like hiring. If the other saying was "Opposites attract except when they absolutely drive one another batty," I could buy it.

☆☆☆☆☆
☆☆☆☆☆
☆☆☆☆☆
☆☆☆☆☆
☆☆☆☆☆
☆☆☆☆☆
☆☆☆☆☆

By way of specific example, describe for us the methods you use to build relationships with the people who most impact your work.

Answer: Really another way to go about getting an answer to this question of building a relationship. And, this again, may not be a question that initially gives you the specific example of what you are looking for. You may, instead, get the "theoretical" explanation of "relationship dynamics." Ask follow-up questions until you're satisfied you have an answer allowing you to analyze the candidate's attributes. Someone with a plan can replicate the plan. You're not really looking for someone to say "A, I do this; B, I do that, C..." What you are looking for is someone who has thought about the intricacies of building a relationship. "I just sort of listen to people," might be a great answer. Or something like "I don't know. I guess I like to hear other people talk about their experiences," is another good clue.

Describe for us a relationship you've had with a person in the past and how it has broken down and then what the outcome was (Follow-up: What did you learn from this process?).

Answer: Asking a negative inquiry to confirm a positive is generally a good approach. Where building relationships is concerned, the most critical skill set, spending the majority of time evaluating whether someone brings the necessary skills to the table is your most important job. We've all had relationships that break from time to time, but our response to those breakages is paramount to our understanding whether we're interviewing someone who can work with a person even though he or she has experienced difficulties or whether we're talking with a person who is real good at holding on to the past—these sorts of folks we simply do not need in our workplace.

Customer Service Skills

Right next to "Relationship Building Skills" for the Teller Model I built was his or her ability to build and grow a relationship with customers. Exceptional Tellers really enjoy the challenge of dealing with people on a variety of issues, some difficult. You'll find anyone who faces the customer in his or her job will need this skill as well. These people covet the opportunity to serve their customers. They genuinely care about the people who are their customers and talk of them in terms of "family."

People who are successful at customer service also spend more time with their customers than is demanded by the task they must perform (for example, someone comes in to cash a check and our exceptional Teller may take a few minutes to talk to the customer about his or her family).

What is most interesting about this process is these Tellers have the highest rates of production of any of the employee groups they're in. Therefore, although they're spending the time necessary to build a relationship, they're going much faster at processing transactions than their counterparts. The ability to spend this time, to build these relationships, does not negatively impact the exceptional performer's production, but actually appears to enhance it.

Here are clues that may help you assess this vital role. Watch for eye contact (although be cognizant of the fact that some cultures discourage eye contact, finding eye contact to be a sign of disrespect and finding averting the eyes to be a sign of respect).

Does the candidate remember and call you by name? Does the candidate seem to smile easily? Does the candidate wait for you to finish your question before answering? Does the candidate project a professional, confident image?

Subtle clues that can assist (not overpower) your assessment.

NOTE: Someone straight out of high school where we are their first employer may have difficulty with the concept of "customer" and "customer service." Generally, someone who has GREAT relationship building skills will build great rapport with our customers. Also, there may be other "customers" "kids" have had, like teachers, peers or parents, but we sort of have to watch getting into personal areas unrelated to work and therefore I am a proponent of this approach only if we use some fairly significant care.

Following are a few queries that may assist in evaluating someone's ability to build customer relationships:

Describe for us a specific example of a good customer you have worked with over the years and how you developed this relationship with this person.

☆☆☆☆☆
☆☆☆☆☆
☆☆☆☆☆
☆☆☆☆☆
☆☆☆☆☆
☆☆☆☆☆
☆☆☆☆☆
☆☆☆☆☆

Answer: Exemplary employees describe their difficult customers as "demanding" or "a little toot," or something even less flattering and more corny, but they very rarely seek the really derogatory descriptors of a problem customer: "He's a moron," or "She's so retarded" (which have a bunch of problems at several levels not the least of which is language like "moron," or "retard" shows someone who is ignorant of their obvious prejudice toward groups of people).

Don't hire these disrespectful people. They're disrespectful of a group of people, or a coworker, or a customer, or you.

If we know our customers, we should be able to compare the "good" customer our candidate describes to our customer base and see if there are similarities. Watch for someone who equates good with easy. Some of the best relationships can be built with folks who are not the easiest to deal with.

As an employee, this sort of person, the one who fixes things even with the customer who isn't easy, is the exact sort of person you want on your side as part of your employee group.

Tell us how you build a relationship with a customer using a specific example to illustrate.

Answer: This will be a difficult question for most folks to answer. They'll probably get the theoretical side of the question answered, but have difficulty bridging from theoretical to practical. You may have to ask a follow-up or two to get to a good, usable answer.

☆ ☆ ☆ ☆ ☆ _____
☆ ☆ ☆ ☆ ☆ _____
☆ ☆ ☆ ☆ ☆ _____
☆ ☆ ☆ ☆ ☆ _____
☆ ☆ ☆ ☆ ☆ _____
☆ ☆ ☆ ☆ ☆ _____
☆ ☆ ☆ ☆ ☆ _____

We should be seeking people who have some sort of a plan. The "oh, I don't know, it just sort of happens" is an interesting approach, but not one that can be replicated in a variety of situations. Truth be told, too, the folks who use the preceding are probably reluctant to talk about themselves and their successes. Some of these folks have some real definite ways they influence the growth of their customer relationships, they simply have never been asked this question.

Dig a little and you may get to a usable answer. Customer service is paramount to the exceptional Teller's performance. Building a great relationship with his or her customer is the first step toward achieving this performance.

At a minimum, if they have a plan, their plan should include listening, discovering all the facts and sharing pertinent information. "Problem solving" may be in there somewhere, but problem solving is a broad concept; you're more interested in understanding what they mean by that—how do they solve a problem—so ask—the next most difficult question:

"I know what I mean when I say "problem solving," but give me a specific example that shows me what you mean." I'll talk more about "the next most difficult question, the follow-up, in the final chapter.

Tell us about a specific example or two where a customer came to you with a problem and how you worked to resolve the problem.

Answer: Great employees are problem solvers. There's a sign at Winter Park Ski Resort. As you're swooshing down the mountain on a pristine slope of powder and thinking about "kicking it up a notch," you look up and see this sign "Know Your Limit. Ski Within It." Great employees solve the problems they have the authority to solve and take the rest to the next level and they know the difference.

Taking an issue to a supervisor isn't a bad thing. What determines whether this decision was a good one is whether the level of the problem deserved the level of the solution.

Great employees ski within their limits.

These employees view problems not as big deals, but rather as opportunities to help someone. This is the sort of person we should be seeking when we're attempting to hire virtually anyone. Listen for how the candidate works to solve a problem and how big a problem the customer had to begin with. If the problem doesn't seem like that big a deal "well, one of my customers found $100 outside the door and didn't know how he was going to spend it," or the solution seems vague "we just sort of talked it out," then ask a follow-up or two "okay, that's sort of a fun problem, but now think back to a fairly serious issue a customer had and how you went about solving that issue."

Don't hesitate to keep asking follow-up questions until you're exhausted or you have an answer you can use—either way, you'll probably be able to make a hiring decision.

Tell us about a specific example or two where a customer brought you a problem and you were unable to solve the problem and what the resolution for the customer was. (Follow-up: Did this customer

☆☆☆☆☆
☆☆☆☆☆
☆☆☆☆☆
☆☆☆☆☆
☆☆☆☆☆
☆☆☆☆☆
☆☆☆☆☆

continue to be a customer? Why [do you think]? or Why not [do you think]?)

Answer: Exceptional employees know their limits in terms of problem solving and do not hesitate to bring a supervisor into the equation, providing the supervisor with adequate background and explanations of the solutions that have been offered. At the same time, some problems do not yield themselves to positive outcomes.

A customer who has made a decimal point error, again, in his or her checking account is probably not going to be overjoyed when a Teller points out this problem to him or her and the bank is unwilling to waive the insufficient charges.

These are the sorts of problems great employees handle with empathy and apologies and often maintain a customer relationship by providing future support in "double-checking" the math [or whatever]. Others may have a tendency to lose a customer because they respond in kind with a curt, uncaring, or incorrect response.

Give us a specific example of where you influenced a customer's decision, perhaps in a purchase of a product, and why you feel you were able to influence that decision.

Answer: Most employees do not consider themselves sales people in the traditional sense. Exceptional employees tend to believe themselves to be "helpers" and "persuaders" and can sell exceptionally well using these techniques to influence customer decisions.

☆ ☆ ☆ ☆ ☆
☆ ☆ ☆ ☆ ☆
☆ ☆ ☆ ☆ ☆
☆ ☆ ☆ ☆ ☆
☆ ☆ ☆ ☆ ☆
☆ ☆ ☆ ☆ ☆
☆ ☆ ☆ ☆ ☆
☆ ☆ ☆ ☆ ☆

These employees have no qualms about making suggestions that will benefit our customers and thus enhance the long-term relationships that yield the highest profits. They are not doing this to necessarily positively impact the bottom-line; they're doing this to help a customer, their friend.

This question, though, is incredibly difficult to answer. This can be a tough question, but look for some selling skills. Again, these are listening, empathy, but also a willingness to suggest some alternatives that make sense and benefit the customer. And, remember, always, persistence is the key to almost anything; a "failure" is often someone who quits trying.

By way of a specific example illustrate for us what "customer service" means to you. What we are asking is for you to give us an example of a one-on-one with a customer that will allow us to see your definition of customer service. (NOTE: This can be a very difficult question.)

 Answer: What makes this question so difficult is not the content, but the context. What we are asking someone to do is to give us a definition by drawing us a verbal picture. This may or may not yield a good result and you may have to work long and hard to get to a usable answer, but the work may be most worthwhile as someone who defines their customer service through example will give you an absolute view of how they handle customers. Others will simply provide a textbook definition of sorts that you may or may not agree with.

☆☆☆☆☆ _____
☆☆☆☆☆ _____
☆☆☆☆☆ _____
☆☆☆☆☆ _____
☆☆☆☆☆ _____
☆☆☆☆☆ _____
☆☆☆☆☆ _____

Tell us about a time you've had to work with a really irate, or unreasonable, customer and what the outcome was and how you attempted to handle this customer.

Answer: Ask the negative to confirm the positive. You should get a picture of how the candidate works with a great customer, but we also want a picture of how the candidate works with difficult people. You're really looking to exclude the know-it-all, or the person who doesn't seem to listen to the customer, or the person who pretends to care. You may be surprised at the information some candidates are willing to share. Some of these surprises are of the "what a wonderful surprise" variety; most are not.

Again, using a specific example, show us how you have handled a dissatisfied customer in the past.

Answer: Another way of attacking the preceding question. Working with difficult people is a part of almost any job. How someone is able to handle these situations probably determines whether he or she is simply successful or has the capacity to be one of your exceptional performers.

In looking at your past relationships with customers, tell us what steps you would take to improve the level of service you provide. (Follow-ups: Have you taken these steps already, or are these things you would do? Why do you think this course of action will work? Or, "Describe how this course of action worked." Tell us about a specific example that illustrates how you enhanced your customer service in the way you just described).

☆ ☆ ☆ ☆ ☆
☆ ☆ ☆ ☆ ☆
☆ ☆ ☆ ☆ ☆
☆ ☆ ☆ ☆ ☆
☆ ☆ ☆ ☆ ☆
☆ ☆ ☆ ☆ ☆
☆ ☆ ☆ ☆ ☆
☆ ☆ ☆ ☆ ☆

Answer: You're really asking two questions here. First, you should get a lot of information about how the candidate has worked with customers in the past. This information you can use in your analysis by comparing it to your Model you developed for the position you're hiring for. At the same time you want someone who is constantly improving his or her skill sets.

What do you like least about providing customer service? Why? Please provide us with an example.

Answer: Usually, especially with less mature [not age, but maturity level] individuals, we'll get "I just love everything about customer service."

You'll need to follow-up for a legitimate answer. Be looking for things candidates do not like to do, but are required of the position for which you are hiring.

As a Teller, the bank wouldn't hire someone who doesn't enjoy handling money, but in the past we've sometimes hired people who don't enjoy working with others, or who don't have a basic understanding of how to follow rules.

Look for elements in this answer that are telltale signs of things someone may not like to do. If a core responsibility of your job is something this person doesn't appear inclined to enjoy, move on to the next candidate. Don't hesitate to ask a follow-up question, the next most difficult question.

☆☆☆☆☆
☆☆☆☆☆
☆☆☆☆☆
☆☆☆☆☆
☆☆☆☆☆
☆☆☆☆☆
☆☆☆☆☆

Describe for us a time when you have performed at what you consider to be above and beyond the call of duty to meet the needs of a customer or client? (Possible follow-up, although somewhat leading: Why did you choose to perform in this way?)

Answer: Not surprisingly, exceptional employees perform at this level as their standard. We should be seeking people who can pull these answers out of the air rather quickly with the following caveat.

If this is someone's standard operating paradigm, he or she may not realize that their "day at work" is an "oh wow!" moment in our world and we have to dig just a little. However, the depth of this query makes it pretty exceptional in terms of a quick "includer," or "excluder."

Someone who cannot think of an instance may either have never been in the workforce and therefore not have the experience, or may not have the basic skill sets (or aptitude or desire) to perform at this level.

Tell us about the most frustrating experience you ever had assisting someone. (Follow-ups: Tell us about a situation like this when you handled it well, and one when you did not. What did you do in each case?)

Answer: Another great opportunity to listen for things that someone doesn't like to do. What made this situation so frustrating? Is the level of frustration understandable? How was the frustration handled? Did the candidate seem to lose patience, or did the candidate seem to

☆ ☆ ☆ ☆ ☆ _____

☆ ☆ ☆ ☆ ☆ _____

☆ ☆ ☆ ☆ ☆ _____

☆ ☆ ☆ ☆ ☆ _____

☆ ☆ ☆ ☆ ☆ _____

☆ ☆ ☆ ☆ ☆ _____

☆ ☆ ☆ ☆ ☆ _____

☆ ☆ ☆ ☆ ☆ _____

maintain his or her composure? Was the situation brought to a successful conclusion?

We like to think all of our customers are reasonable and wonderful people. However, in this job you will be interacting with a variety of individuals within our Bank as well as outside of our Bank. Occasionally, you will interact with a customer that is dissatisfied with the service he or she received. Tell us about the most difficult customer you have encountered in your current or past jobs and how you worked to handle his or her problem. (NOTE: You've given the candidate a lot of information and maybe loaded the answer. Generally, when asking a question, the less background information you can give, the better.)

Answer: A similar question has been asked before. The answer is similar: Ask the negative to confirm the positive. You should get a picture of how the candidate works with a great customer, but we also want a picture of how the candidate works with difficult people.

You're really looking to exclude the know-it-all, or the person who doesn't seem to listen to the customer, or the person who pretends to care.

Tell us about the last time you went out of your way to help a customer, include what you did and why you chose to do this.

Answer: Again a similar query has been asked before and the answer is essentially the same. Exceptional employees perform at this level as their standard.

☆ ☆ ☆ ☆ ☆
☆ ☆ ☆ ☆ ☆
☆ ☆ ☆ ☆ ☆
☆ ☆ ☆ ☆ ☆
☆ ☆ ☆ ☆ ☆
☆ ☆ ☆ ☆ ☆
☆ ☆ ☆ ☆ ☆

Seek people who can pull these answers out of the air rather quickly with the following caveat. If this is someone's standard operating paradigm, he or she may not realize that their "day at work" is an "oh wow!" moment in our world and we have to dig just a little.

Unlike the last query that had this response, this one probably doesn't have enough depth to count as a "quick" includer or "excluder." Someone who cannot think of an instance may either have never been in the workforce and therefore not have the experience, or may not have the basic skill sets [or aptitude or desire] to perform at this level.

Describe for us a situation where you were asked a question by a customer and you did not know the answer. (NOTE: You may need to follow-up on this one as you're not looking for the situation, but rather how the candidate responded to the situation.)

Answer: A seemingly simple question that answers whether this candidate knows when it is time to bring in a person able to solve a customer's problem. Exceptional employees know to turn to their supervisor at appropriate times.

They do not take trivia to a supervisor, but have no qualms about contacting a supervisor if they're having trouble maintaining a customer relationship, or adequately dealing with a customer problem. In other words, they don't allow their egos to stand in the way of exceptional customer service.

Tell us about the most difficult problem you had with a customer and how it was resolved.

☆ ☆ ☆ ☆ ☆
☆ ☆ ☆ ☆ ☆
☆ ☆ ☆ ☆ ☆
☆ ☆ ☆ ☆ ☆
☆ ☆ ☆ ☆ ☆
☆ ☆ ☆ ☆ ☆
☆ ☆ ☆ ☆ ☆
☆ ☆ ☆ ☆ ☆

Answer: Similar questions to this have been asked twice before. The answer is similar: Ask the negative to confirm the positive. You should get a picture of how the candidate works with a great customer, but we also want a picture of how the candidate works with difficult people. You're really looking to exclude the know-it-all, or the person who doesn't seem to listen to the customer, or the person who pretends to care.

People Skills (the ability to love people)

Dividing "Relationship Building Skills," "Customer Service" and this "People Skills" into separate skill sets is a difficult task. There is a great degree of overlap in all three skill set areas.

When talking with exceptional employees, "People Skills," a genuine desire to be with people, seemed to drive their work. As with "Customer Service Skills" look for the other, body language, clues. Someone who seems uncomfortable with you, even in the discomfort of an interview, may be exhibiting some of these traits that make them uncomfortable around people—exceptional performers are extremely comfortable, or get comfortable, in almost all settings with a wide variety of people.

That to say, you will still run across folks who are simply monumentally uncomfortable in an interview setting. Please do not discount someone because they don't fit that "extremely comfortable." You may be tossing out an exceptional performer.

☆☆☆☆☆
☆☆☆☆☆
☆☆☆☆☆
☆☆☆☆☆
☆☆☆☆☆
☆☆☆☆☆
☆☆☆☆☆

The following are questions that should help you ascertain the candidate's skill level in this area:

Tell us about the best group of people you've ever worked with and what made this the best group.

Answer: There's a story that made the rounds of leadership groups many years ago. Basically a lady is sitting at a train station and a train pulls up and a man gets off and says "I'm looking for a great town. Is this town a great town?" The lady says "what sort of town did you leave?" The man goes on and on about the horrible town he's leaving. The lady says "well, this town is a lot similar and I'd suggest you keep looking." The man re-boards the train and leaves the town.

Another day, another train pulls in and another man gets off the train and says to this same lady "I'm looking for a great town. Is this that sort of town?" The lady again asks "what sort of town did you leave?" The man says "oh, a wonderful town. I hated to leave. Great people." The lady says "Welcome. You've found another town just like that one."

This question asks the candidate to describe what he or she sees as far as their town. Someone who has had horrid coworkers and terrible supervisors and an awful environment is possibly going to find the same here because the problem with horrible situations is often not in the people or situations at all, but within us and that doesn't change because we get on a train and go somewhere else.

☆ ☆ ☆ ☆ ☆
☆ ☆ ☆ ☆ ☆
☆ ☆ ☆ ☆ ☆
☆ ☆ ☆ ☆ ☆
☆ ☆ ☆ ☆ ☆
☆ ☆ ☆ ☆ ☆
☆ ☆ ☆ ☆ ☆
☆ ☆ ☆ ☆ ☆

Obviously this question doesn't ask the candidate to describe a terrible work group, but rather the best, but many times negative people end up describing negative things. Don't be surprised when you ask a positive and get a negative. That's what negative people do.

Describe for us a group where you just really didn't click and why you believe this was not your group.

Answer: Here's where you're going to start gathering a lot of good information in regards to how this person views the world. We've all had relationships that we'd just as soon not have, but these should be exceptions rather than the rule.

Listen. Don't interrupt. Allow for silence and you'll get some good information. Remember the story of the train and the town from the preceding query.

Tell us about a specific customer you met for the first time and why you remember him or her.

Answer: You're looking for the things this person found important in meeting this customer and whether unimportant things played for or against establishing a relationship.

Stellar employees see almost all customers as potential people worth meeting, friends possibly. They immediately start developing a relationship.

☆☆☆☆☆
☆☆☆☆☆
☆☆☆☆☆
☆☆☆☆☆
☆☆☆☆☆
☆☆☆☆☆
☆☆☆☆☆

You should feel this from your candidate, even at the point of the interview. Ask yourself a simple question immediately after the interview: "Did I like this person?"

Being likable is an interesting science, and you can hire for it, but there's not a question I can suggest, or a test you can give that's going to answer that question.

I can tell you something you already know: Being around folks you like is a lot easier than being around folks you dislike. We should always hire employees we like. Always. ALWAYS.

Describe for us a profile of the customers you currently work with (how old are they, what is their sex, in other words what is their demographic make-up). (Follow-up: Tell us how you treat these different customers and why you choose to treat them differently or choose not to treat them with a great deal of difference).

Answer: One other aspect of success in an exceptional employee's portfolio is the ability to profile a customer and remember attributes about him or her (name, family, kids in school, etc.).

Exceptional employees tend to segregate customers and treat each individually knowing the folks they can sort of joke around with and knowing the customers who require a gentler, guiding hand.

You may get a lot of "oh, I treat everyone the same," which has become something of a mantra with all the litigation companies face,

☆ ☆ ☆ ☆ ☆
☆ ☆ ☆ ☆ ☆
☆ ☆ ☆ ☆ ☆
☆ ☆ ☆ ☆ ☆
☆ ☆ ☆ ☆ ☆
☆ ☆ ☆ ☆ ☆
☆ ☆ ☆ ☆ ☆
☆ ☆ ☆ ☆ ☆

but we're really looking for someone who segregates people not based on nonsense factors, but based on character and personality and the customer's individual needs. And based on an understanding that there are generational and cultural differences that shouldn't work to separate us, but do help to make us unique.

Describe for us some of the traits in coworkers you find most agreeable.

Answer: This and the next question sort of takes the group dynamic down to the individual. You should be able to take the candidate's likes and dislikes and compare them to the group you have and then decide if the candidate is a "fit." At the same time, you may be attempting to change some of your group dynamics.

Maybe you have a group that likes to sort of get into cliques. Getting someone who not only abhors this behavior, but has demonstrated from past examples a desire to break up cliques may be just the type of person to introduce to this group. Ignoring things is easy; addressing them in a politically sensitive manner takes guts and fortitude. Beware, however, as you are probably responsible for how your group performs.

If you critically analyze this and come to the conclusion, "Hey, it's me," I would advocate not putting someone completely different into a situation where they're probably destined to fail and hate the time they spend doing it.

☆ ☆ ☆ ☆ ☆
☆ ☆ ☆ ☆ ☆
☆ ☆ ☆ ☆ ☆
☆ ☆ ☆ ☆ ☆
☆ ☆ ☆ ☆ ☆
☆ ☆ ☆ ☆ ☆
☆ ☆ ☆ ☆ ☆

In other words we sometimes simply have to fix ourselves to fix our group (and that's not to suggest we can fix a low performer by becoming more "tolerant" of unacceptable results).

Describe for us some of the traits in coworkers you perhaps don't feel are that appealing.

Answer: Most of us don't like to talk badly about others, especially in an interview. But usually there are some things we don't like about others. Like maybe we don't like someone without a sense of humor. Whatever comes up is probably just the surface, that is "the most safe" response.

You may need to follow-up with something like "well, just expand on that further for me." Again, being quiet and patient will probably yield some additional information as the candidate will know you are waiting for something and folks tend to become more comfortable with a longer interview and that's going to drive their desire to give you a complete answer and we all tend to become uncomfortable with dead space, which, by the way, cuts both ways and can work against us as the interviewer. We have to get real comfortable with dead space and silence.

Describe for us something a coworker has done in the past that has upset you and how you responded to this situation.

Answer: Again, one of those questions that people hate to answer, but be looking for "the rest of the story" by again being patient and quiet. Follow-up if you have to. Your mission is to be able to compare the

☆ ☆ ☆ ☆ ☆
☆ ☆ ☆ ☆ ☆
☆ ☆ ☆ ☆ ☆
☆ ☆ ☆ ☆ ☆
☆ ☆ ☆ ☆ ☆
☆ ☆ ☆ ☆ ☆
☆ ☆ ☆ ☆ ☆
☆ ☆ ☆ ☆ ☆

unknown (the candidate's likes and dislikes) to the more known (your group's and your company's likes and dislikes as defined by your Model).

When you decide to do something on your own, is it usually something like watch television by yourself, read a good book, go to a movie with a friend, or do something with a group of people, or something different than one of our examples? (Follow-up: Tells us why you decide to do what you do and not some other thing.)(NOTE: The preceding list is not work-related, so be careful if you choose to ask this question. Also, realize you're still looking for a specific example, not just an "oh, I'd watch television" sort of response. This question, too, is getting somewhat into the "if you were a tree, what sort of tree would you be?" type of query, so you may or may not get usable information from it.) Good advice as well if they say "read," is to ask what book and what they liked about it. I don't know why, but a lot of folks seem to say "read" and haven't read a book in years.

Answer: Again, please be a little careful with this one as this can lead into some non-work-related and more legally questionable and legally significant areas. You're almost always safe if your questions and the responses you receive are strictly related to work and work activities.

This, however, can be a good query to determine whether someone likes to curl up in a corner with a book and a warm blanket (nothing wrong with this behavior by the way), or whether someone prefers the company of others. Exceptional customer facing employees are generally social people and prefer the company of others, although I'm sure several of them like to curl up with a good book from time to time

☆ ☆ ☆ ☆ ☆ _____
☆ ☆ ☆ ☆ ☆ _____
☆ ☆ ☆ ☆ ☆ _____
☆ ☆ ☆ ☆ ☆ _____
☆ ☆ ☆ ☆ ☆ _____
☆ ☆ ☆ ☆ ☆ _____
☆ ☆ ☆ ☆ ☆ _____

as well. Their dominant trait is to be with other people. This is what you should be hiring in a customer-facing position.

Communication Skills

All of these skill sets tie to one another. Communication seemed to be one of the "harder" skills (if the others can be described as "softer"). Building great relationships, performing great customer service and having good people skills all seemed to grow out of an ability to communicate.

Those Tellers who were not as fluent in English or who were not as good at writing simply seemed to work harder in the other areas to accommodate this generally recognized "weakness."

The following are questions that can assist in analyzing someone's ability to communicate (the application and/or resume [if required] may also yield some possible clues):

Describe for us the most difficult person you have ever had to have a conversation with and what made this so difficult and what the outcome was.

Answer: Dealing one-on-one with another person regarding a negative situation is probably one of the hardest tasks any of us have ever been asked, or have ever needed, to perform.

People who have never done this are coach-able, so just because someone fresh out of high school has never had such an encounter doesn't mean to scratch him or her off the list. But what this probably does suggest is that these folks will require quite a bit of training to get up to speed in this critical area.

You're really looking to exclude folks who have had the opportunity to have these sorts of conversations and haven't taken them, or have repeatedly handled them poorly thus failing to learn, or work to avoid these sorts of conversations to the point of allowing a problem to fester into a big issue, or to the point of "solving" the problem without involving the parties.

Tell us about a customer phone call you've received where understanding the problem was difficult and how you went about first discovering what the problem was then responding to it.

Answer: Listening is the key to understanding. That's what you're looking for in an exceptional performer—the ability to actively listen. Be looking for the person who perhaps snaps too quickly or gives too quick an answer.

Another good way to answer this question is to look at your interview and look at how this candidate has responded to you. Did he or she think about a response before answering? Did he or she answer your questions? Did he or she ask for clarification, if the candidate appeared not to understand? These are the sorts of attributes of a great communicator. Someone who simply talks a lot isn't necessarily communicating; he or she is just using words and oxygen.

☆☆☆☆☆
☆☆☆☆☆
☆☆☆☆☆
☆☆☆☆☆
☆☆☆☆☆
☆☆☆☆☆
☆☆☆☆☆

By way of illustration and example, show us what you consider to be the most important aspect in the communication process and why you consider this to be the most important.

Answer: By far the most important aspect of communication is active listening. Someone cannot diagnose and address a problem, if he fails to listen to the problem. There will be very few candidates who say "active listening." But what you are looking for is an understanding that a doctor does not prescribe before he or she has a diagnosis. What this means is listening allows us to understand a problem and then work toward a mutually understood (not necessarily agreeable) solution.

Give me an example of the most complex communication problem you ever faced. (Possible follow-ups: What made it the most complex? What made the communication so difficult? How could you have improved the communication? How did you solve this problem and why? How effective were your communications?)

Answer: What you're looking for here is the depth of the candidate's understanding and how nimble he or she is in creatively looking for resolutions. Exceptional employees face difficult problems as opportunity; others may see them only as obstacles.

Over the years replacing "problem" with "opportunity" became a product of leadership training as we "changed our vocabulary." Realizing of course not many of us see a car wreck and think "oh, they sure have some opportunity." These exceptional employees may still call a problem a problem, but their approach is toward an opportunity.

☆ ☆ ☆ ☆ ☆
☆ ☆ ☆ ☆ ☆
☆ ☆ ☆ ☆ ☆
☆ ☆ ☆ ☆ ☆
☆ ☆ ☆ ☆ ☆
☆ ☆ ☆ ☆ ☆
☆ ☆ ☆ ☆ ☆
☆ ☆ ☆ ☆ ☆

Exceptional employees also seem to know when they need to include a supervisor in the process.

When faced with a very irate or extremely difficult customer, tell us, by way of specific example, how you go about attempting to deal with the customer and solve the problem. This query is a little leading with "solve the problem" and you may simply want to end it after "customer." (Follow-up: How successful are you using this strategy? What examples can you tell us about that tend to support this conclusion?)

Answer: "We apologize profusely" was easily the number one response I've received in almost every interview I've ever conducted with an exceptional employee. "I immediately say I'm sorry" to an upset or unreasonable customer.

Even if the customer seemed to be "wrong," exceptional employees tended to shoulder the responsibility for the problem and then work with the customer so that the customer would better understand where he or she made the mistake. There did not seem to be a huge need for these great employees to be "right."

Empathy was their guiding principle.

Tell us about something you have written that has given you the results you desired. This may be a letter to a customer, a letter of complaint to another company, a memo to a supervisor, or an e-mail. Simply pick a specific example and describe what results you wanted and what the response was to your written documentation.

☆☆☆☆☆ _____
☆☆☆☆☆ _____
☆☆☆☆☆ _____
☆☆☆☆☆ _____
☆☆☆☆☆ _____
☆☆☆☆☆ _____
☆☆☆☆☆ _____

Answer: We are simply wanting to insure someone we're hiring knows how to write a semi-coherent, semi-complete sentence. Those who do not know how to accomplish this goal are occasionally also the ones having difficulty with their paperwork and following procedures (because an inability to write is occasionally also an inability [or lack of desire] to read and more importantly understand).

Tell us about a specific incident where you have apologized to a customer for something that you didn't consider to be exactly your or your company's fault.

Answer: As I mentioned earlier, "I apologize profusely" was easily the number one response exceptional employees give to an upset or unreasonable customer. We should, therefore, try to determine whether our candidate has this capacity to empathize, apologize and fix the problem.

Problem Solving Skills

I would hazard to guess that all exceptional employees are problem solvers. They are faced with a multitude of problems throughout the day. The Tellers I interviewed saw everything from making a decision on cashing a check, to tracking down history, to determining where an error was made in someone's account and all of this becomes the domain of the Teller.

Exceptional employees are better at achieving a good resolution even to a negative situation. The following questions may assist in evaluating a candidate's potential at becoming an exceptional employee and his or her ability to solve problems.

Describe for us the customer who brought to you the most difficult problem you can recall and what made this so difficult and what the outcome was.

Answer: This is a fairly difficult question. You are looking for the "most difficult problem" and this may take some effort on the part of the candidate.

Exceptional employees unbelievably like problems. They face these things as challenges and they tend to invigorate these unique employees.

As I mentioned a moment ago, many years ago, business people replaced "problem" with "opportunity," so now everyone, or a lot of people, see an obstacle, but for political astuteness call it an "opportunity."

Exceptional employees still often times refer to these as "problems," but they seem to approach them as opportunity. They haven't switched their vocabulary and their predisposition has always been to see "problems" as "opportunities."

Provide us with a specific example of your problem-solving ability.

Answer: A pretty short, but potentially telling query. A person good at solving problems does so through the use of some logical, ordered structure. They may never have thought about that logical process so coming up with an answer may take some effort, but their response should include some of the following: (1) they listen, (2) they may summarize what they have heard, (3) they empathize and potentially apologize, (4) they separate the problem from the customer and become partners with the customer in dealing with the problem, (5) they investigate from several different angles to ensure they are solving the right problem, (6) they bring in other experts (supervisors), if necessary, (7) they propose a solution, (8) they modify and execute their solution, and (9) they check back to see if they solved the right problem and didn't create new ones.

We should be looking for folks who maybe don't follow this 9-step regimen, but at least have a plan they do follow, and it probably contains, in one form or fashion, some of the preceding elements.

Tell us about a situation you were involved in where you had to solve a problem and how you went about solving this problem.

Answer: See the preceding query's answer as this question is very much similar. Again, you are looking for a specific example from their past.

You may want to ask several questions about problem solving and the candidate may be inclined to point back to the preceding answer as in "well, as I explained, when I was dealing…" Therefore, you may want to preface a second and subsequent question with "I know you've already talked to me about a problem you dealt with, but for this next question I want you to use a different specific example and "Tell us…"

These questions, as you have probably already deduced, are not easy and may take the candidate some time to formulate a response. Silence and time are not enemies to the process. Where appropriate, I would recommend using both liberally.

Show us, by way of example, what you do when a customer first brings a problem to your attention.

Answer: Exceptional employees enjoy communication and enjoy problem solving. They understand they cannot solve a problem without listening to what the problem is. The first step toward solving a problem is therefore listening and this is what this answer should suggest.

☆☆☆☆☆
☆☆☆☆☆
☆☆☆☆☆
☆☆☆☆☆
☆☆☆☆☆
☆☆☆☆☆
☆☆☆☆☆

Someone who proposes quick solutions may be solving the wrong problem, although many managers are impressed by this "quick problem solver." "I'm a real fast problem solver," may, but not necessarily, point to this trait. Again, you want someone who does an adequate diagnosis before going after a prescription.

Tell us what steps you take when you are not able to solve a problem.

Answer: You will not get a behavioral answer when the candidate first responds and this is okay. Usually what they will say is "they go to their supervisor."

After they respond, ask them for a specific example: "think of an example where you took a problem to your supervisor and kind of walk us through what happened." You seek not only information on whether the person follows through to the conclusion of a problem (exceptional employees do), but whether the problem's difficulty seemed to warrant involvement of a supervisor.

Describe for us a specific example on any job you have ever held when you were faced with a customer problem that tested your problem-solving skills.

Answer: You should get a behavioral response, but you may not necessarily receive one. You may, therefore, need to follow-up with "What did you do?" to get to a better answer. You're looking for someone who has spent some time thinking about problem solving. Getting to the right solution may not be that big a deal at the level your candidate is at, but having an understanding of a process is important.

☆ ☆ ☆ ☆ ☆
☆ ☆ ☆ ☆ ☆
☆ ☆ ☆ ☆ ☆
☆ ☆ ☆ ☆ ☆
☆ ☆ ☆ ☆ ☆
☆ ☆ ☆ ☆ ☆
☆ ☆ ☆ ☆ ☆
☆ ☆ ☆ ☆ ☆

This is what this question is testing—do they have, or have they thought of, the process?

Provide us an example of a time when you were dealing with a customer and had to make a quick decision.

Answer: A really tough question simply from the standpoint that most folks at many levels may not think they have been in a decision-making capacity. However they probably make decisions all the time, but just don't think about them.

Exceptional employees, like the Tellers I interviewed, point to pretty casual tasks, check cashing, as part of their decision-making tree— "should I, or should I not cash this check?" The people who become outstanding employees probably recognize decisions they make in a different light than a casual observer would. They quickly understand that they're solving problems constantly.

Discuss with us a difficult situation you have had with a supervisor in the past and how you handled it.

Answer: Wow, what a mother-lode of information this question could potentially reveal. You will have candidates who profess to never having a problem with a supervisor. You may have to follow-up with "Well, just think about it for a bit because all of us have had a concern we have brought to a manager's attention.

You want to also explore the outcomes. You want people who will work a problem. You'll have candidates who say "I wasn't comfortable talking to this supervisor about it, so I found another job." You'll also find candidates who walk you through a real good decision-making process. The "finding another job" may actually be a good resolution to the problem depending on the gravity, or perceived gravity, of the situation, so don't write someone off because he or she chose to leave an untenable situation.

Ability to Follow Rules and/or Procedures

None, count them, zero, of the Tellers I interviewed *focused* on "following rules." I also haven't found a lot of other exceptional employees who were "rules oriented." Generally I have found this trait stronger in those employees who have recently moved from their previous position to management and I find these conversations interesting not only from this aspect, but also because these employees have already gained some political astuteness and their answers have become somewhat guarded.

A little more of trying to guess what I wanted to hear. This is a very interesting transformation that generally occurs in employees as they "move up" in an organization. Where rules came into play for those I interviewed was in the overall scheme of doing their jobs.

Tell us about a policy or procedure you disagreed with at one of your previous employers and how you handled this disagreement.

☆ ☆ ☆ ☆ ☆
☆ ☆ ☆ ☆ ☆
☆ ☆ ☆ ☆ ☆
☆ ☆ ☆ ☆ ☆
☆ ☆ ☆ ☆ ☆
☆ ☆ ☆ ☆ ☆
☆ ☆ ☆ ☆ ☆
☆ ☆ ☆ ☆ ☆

Answer: This question can be framed with a person who recently graduated from high school by adding "or in school," if they do not have any work experience.

If someone doesn't know what the policies of their preceding employer were, be careful; they should have some idea. Otherwise the candidate either didn't think they were important or the organization didn't think they were important—usually the candidate didn't think the rules to be important enough to read them, but probably followed them, more or less, because that's what most of us do. And, there are businesses that don't focus on rules, but a general rule is "come to work on time," so you may have to explore this a bit.

Don't be looking for someone myopically focused on following rules, but you do want someone who is cognizant of the fact that all workplaces have rules and they're willing to follow most of them for the most part.

Tell us about a policy or procedure, that one of your previous employers had, you thought was real good and why you thought this to be a good policy or procedure.

Answer: Really simply the flipside of the preceding question. Listen for what the candidate liked about this policy and why he or she felt it was worthwhile. "I really liked the vacation policy" is usually said in jest, but it may be worth exploring just to determine what sort of level of excitement the employee has about "time off."

☆☆☆☆☆
☆☆☆☆☆
☆☆☆☆☆
☆☆☆☆☆
☆☆☆☆☆
☆☆☆☆☆
☆☆☆☆☆

You really are not interested in the policies your candidate liked or disliked, but the reasons behind their like or dislike. This can be sort of telling from the standpoint of whether they generally tend to follow policies or they sort of reluctantly go along with things.

You probably won't get anyone who will admit to violating a policy or procedure. And, again, you're looking to compare this person's general outlook with what your organization requires in terms of adherence to policy and procedure. You should have this in your Model especially if "following rules is important to your culture."

Tell us about a time when you were aware that someone was violating a policy and what your response to this was.

Answer: All of us probably know folks who violate policies. Our candidates, depending on their experience, may or may not be able to come up with anything. Again, you're doing something of a reasonableness check.

Also, this is a great test of honesty and a great test of decision making. "Oh, I just sort of let it go" is probably an honest answer; "I took the issue up with my supervisor" is a tad less the norm. If you get this response, I'd recommend trying to flesh out as many details as is possible (When did it happen? What was the supervisor's response? Did your telling the supervisor result in any consequence to your friend [and I use friend purposefully here]? How did this outcome make you feel [even if the supervisor did nothing, the candidate should feel something]).

☆☆☆☆☆
☆☆☆☆☆
☆☆☆☆☆
☆☆☆☆☆
☆☆☆☆☆
☆☆☆☆☆
☆☆☆☆☆
☆☆☆☆☆

One of the best resources we have for evaluating someone's ability or desire to follow rules is in the application process and on the application. I used to exclude people automatically who couldn't follow the instructions I listed in the position posting.

In HR an ability to adhere to rules, since we're often the "policy police" is critical. If I asked for a letter and resume I wanted a letter and resume. This is pretty harsh, but you definitely have a sense of whether the person can follow rules. And, being in human resources, I'm reluctant to hire someone who cannot follow the simple rules. I've grown less reluctant over time, but I still sort of put my antennae up whenever someone fails to follow simple instructions.

Also, look at the application and the "reason for leaving" in particular. "Left for political reasons" is one of my favorites. What was this person a Republican working in a Democratic-dominated workplace? Seriously, all workplaces have some "politics" outside those on a national scale.

Most of us don't even think about them; they're simply part of building and growing relationships. This can also be a clue that there's a policy this person disagreed with. Ask them. This can also be an indication that this person is too immature, or takes things too personally, or has something of a martyr complex.

"I notice on your application that you put you left ACME Bank due to 'political reasons.' List those for me and explain them." You can follow-up "why were these things important to you?" And, I'd recommend starting off with these sorts of questions (although that's contrary to my earlier advice of moving from the general to the specific). Some of this stuff, like leaving a job for "political reasons" is just so stupid I may not continue the interview beyond this answer and I can save a bunch of time.

Most candidates will say something to the effect "oh, you know just office politics." Our immediate response is to nod our approval and therefore agree that this ethereal gaseous mass the candidate just gave us is somehow viable. Do this instead. "Well, I know what I mean when I use the word politics, but I'm trying to determine what that word means to you and why it was important enough that you felt a change in employment was the answer."

If they ask for your meaning say "I think of politics as the Republicans and Democrats and am not sure how I would use that as it relates to work, so is there any way you can help me understand?"

You're asking the next most difficult question, and, "yes," it is hard, and, "yes," it can be uncomfortable, and, "yes," it is necessary—absolutely.

And, anything the candidate puts on his or her application is fair game and I use the application extensively when I'm getting to the end of an interview. I go back and pick it apart and anywhere I pick and have a question, I'm likely to ask about it.

It's a good way to get to the bottom of "was responsible for 175% increase in sales," "managed a workgroup which won 'Team of the

Year,'" and a lot of other things people put on their applications that sound impressive, but may not mean a thing.

"I left because I didn't get along with my supervisor" is another of these "killer reasons" people sometimes put on an application. "Better opportunity" is the usual, but every now and then you get the person wanting to "make a statement." Beware these folks because it's not very eloquent, but they tend to be a pain in the...neck and other places.

Other Attributes

The other attributes listed by our Exceptional Tellers included the following

- Great attitude
- Smile a lot
- Honest
- Not afraid to apologize
- Likes to learn
- Knowledge of products, services, policies and procedures

I haven't developed any questions specific to these because most should come out in the interview and some simply require limited observation to insure what the candidate says is their reality.

A "great attitude" and "smile a lot" should be real evident by the time you finish the interview. If you have doubts ask a question like "Think about the last time you were in a less than good mood and how you worked to improve it and tell us about the circumstance, the mood you were in, what was driving it and how the situation was resolved." That should get you to the information you're seeking (and let's put in that caution about "personal" rather than "business-related;" someone going through a divorce may be in a bad mood, but the divorce isn't any of our business).

Honesty is a pretty tough nut to crack. If we walk up to someone and say "are you honest," their response is invariably "you bet!"

And dishonest people can sell that "you bet" religiously.

I had a manager who once told me he was going to drive from Abilene to Amarillo (about 4 hours) so he could "look him in the eye" when asking another employee about some shenanigans the employee was responsible for. As though "look him in the eye" was going to provide some insight that the manager could glean outside of his crystal ball.

Maybe the stern stare of the manager would break down the employee's defenses and he would leave the building weeping at having been found out. Dishonest folks however don't confess to dishonesty, usually, because we simply ask the question and "look them in the eye."

Much later in this process, and sometimes, we find out a dishonest candidate was being dishonest in their answer. Again, that's what dishonest people do.

☆☆☆☆☆
☆☆☆☆☆
☆☆☆☆☆
☆☆☆☆☆
☆☆☆☆☆
☆☆☆☆☆
☆☆☆☆☆
☆☆☆☆☆

Try a query like "Tell me about the last time you witnessed a coworker (or someone) doing something unethical or dishonest and how you responded to it." They may have difficulty coming up with an answer so you may have to rely on the fall back of "policy violating" to get an answer.

At the same time virtually everyone has taken some "thing" from their employer (be it a Bic pen, or a few sheets of paper, or the color copier upstairs that had been "sitting there for a year"). The small stuff are sort of thought of as "technical dishonesty" things, but you can follow-up with a query like "tell us about a time you had a coworker take anything, even something inconsequential, from your employer?"

Their response to this can be real telling. Most times when people witness stuff like this they sort of shrug their shoulders and move on. We'd like to have folks who don't do this, but sort of figure out a way to resolve the problem. At the same time we're not looking at hiring a bunch of tattletales. And, none of us is perfect, but slight dishonesty can be an indicator that this sort of behavior is "okay," or "not a big deal." At some point some of this stuff becomes a bigger deal—that thought, fortunately for me, is what you have to decide.

However, at this stage of the interview you and the interviewee have become "friends" and don't be surprised if someone offers you up a "bimbo chick" comment related to this whole honesty query.

All the other attributes on this list are pretty hard to measure during an interview. I might recommend they become part of the reference check, but knock me down if anyone is (1) still reading this and (2) actually doing a real thorough reference check.

When you ask the queries that talk about "customer service" you'll probably get a sense for whether the candidate apologizes as part of the process and also get a sense as to whether they feel this is important.

And, going back to a statement I just made...a very low of "low hanging fruit" is the reference check. Not "personal" references necessarily because I've only had one person put someone on their personal references who told me "hire him if you want, but he's about this side of worthless." But business reference checks still yield results even though many managers I've worked with suggest otherwise.

I believe they suggest otherwise because they're not inclined to want to expend this energy or this time.

When I do them I usually can get something and they're using the excuse that "companies don't give out any information" as their excuse.

And, of course, unless they're a current employee, you'll probably not have someone with great knowledge of your products, but, again, the exceptional employees I have interviewed over time do not view this as a skill that is necessary to have on the front-end of the hiring process. Each has used his or her own techniques to learn an entity's products over time. Some have learned better than others. And most have

☆ ☆ ☆ ☆ ☆
☆ ☆ ☆ ☆ ☆
☆ ☆ ☆ ☆ ☆
☆ ☆ ☆ ☆ ☆
☆ ☆ ☆ ☆ ☆
☆ ☆ ☆ ☆ ☆
☆ ☆ ☆ ☆ ☆
☆ ☆ ☆ ☆ ☆

worked for companies that remarkably fail to train them in this critical skill set.

I go back to where I began with a quote from one of the truly exceptional employees I interviewed: "You can learn how to do the ten-key, but never learn how to get a personality."

When I do the hiring I work real, real hard to hire for attitude and train for skill. This isn't even close to my idea, but grumps are just that hard to work with. I've hired them before and I work mighty hard to ensure that if I hire someone who can't do the work at least they're happy; the most competent grump in the world is worse than the most incompetent happy person I've ever had to let go.

A final note, a golden nugget, about interviews. I always (well almost always except where I alluded to getting answers to stupid things out of the way) start an interview with the following: "Start with your most current employer and work back and compare and contrast this employer with your previous employer and what you understand about us. Tell me how your previous jobs relate to our jobs. Tell me what you liked and what you disliked about each workplace and each supervisor."

Maybe the preceding should have come at the beginning of this discussion and not at the end, but I like it at the end as it's not a panacea, but a tactic—a very powerful one—but a tactic nonetheless. It can answer a great many of your interview questions and speed the process and it gives you a very clear picture, a Model, to compare against your Model, of the person you're interviewing.

☆ ☆ ☆ ☆ ☆
☆ ☆ ☆ ☆ ☆
☆ ☆ ☆ ☆ ☆
☆ ☆ ☆ ☆ ☆
☆ ☆ ☆ ☆ ☆
☆ ☆ ☆ ☆ ☆
☆ ☆ ☆ ☆ ☆

And, you'll run across about as many opinions on hiring as there are people in human resources. Do what works for you and your company. I mean I'd probably shy away from the "throw the resumes off the top step and the one closest to the top is our man," but outside of relying solely on a gut feeling, I'd say find your tool and use it.

I know my Model works. I've used it for years and years and years. I know, too, however, that practice makes just about everything better and the same is true of this process. We may wish that we could get in shape by watching the exercise video, but in reality good things take work. This Model concept takes work and there is no video.

Chapter 7
After the
Merry-Go-Round Stops

This near the end of our journey chapter brings in a few other considerations that will work in concert with your Models.

Compensation always seems like a super-big deal because…well, it is, so I'm going to talk a little about compensation and not inconsequentially how you go about paying for the higher cost employee that a Model often represents, or, more accurately, we should be willing to pay for (more on this in a moment).

You certainly don't want to go through all this effort, train an exceptional employee and then lose him or her to competition over a dollar an hour.

The second mini-section of this chapter is a real brief discussion of the interview, taking notes and what not. And, I'm also going to talk about a super-critical thing I alluded to in my discussion of my Teller Model: the next most difficult question.

A Note Regarding Pay

The big question: "Does pay matter?"

The big answer: "Heck yes it matters."

Survey after survey of employees lists "pay" as the reason someone is dissatisfied with their current work or the reason someone leaves a job in the fourth, fifth or lower position on almost any survey. Recently (2016), this seems to have changed and pay has become much more prominent on these types of surveys.

The number one, in the past, was always and easily "supervision," often followed by a "lack of autonomy in decision making," followed by "environment," or "opportunity," or something like that—in other words we could easily conclude "pay simply ain't it. Sorry. It's not."

If we come to this conclusion, based off consolidated survey data, we'd be wrong.

Pay matters. I find ridiculous our apparent acceptance of training our employees and then losing them to competition over a few hundred or a few thousand dollars a year.

For crying out loud, we spent thousands of dollars hiring them, who knows how much training them and making them productive and then we treat $0.50, or $0.75 or shoot $5 an hour as though this were a big decision.

☆☆☆☆☆ _____
☆☆☆☆☆ _____
☆☆☆☆☆ _____
☆☆☆☆☆ _____
☆☆☆☆☆ _____
☆☆☆☆☆ _____
☆☆☆☆☆ _____

If you hire an exceptional employee, and you'll know this fairly quickly, please pay this person appropriately and be proactive about it—don't wait until she comes to you saying "Well, ACME First Federal Credit is going to pay me a dollar more an hour." We should try and insure that if we do lose one of these great employees to ACME, ACME pays a premium. To do otherwise is to shirk our responsibility as leaders in our organization.

To underpay these folks, too, is a slap in their face. The question I've been asked is "well, if you are willing to pay me that much now, why have I been making this much for the last three years?" To which I usually answer "well, um…duh, I dunno," or something similar.

And then they leave more upset than they were when they first started looking (and if you believe the line "I wasn't looking; they called me," I have some ocean front property in Montana I've been trying to unload for a very long time. Call me. I'll make you a deal). Oh, and I really don't answer with "well, um…duh, I dunno," but often feel as though I should.

And, that said, you need to insure you're advocating either a higher rate of pay or a significant increase for only an exceptional performer and not just someone holding a hot hand during their first few months, or someone doing the least most mediocre job.

"But I don't have in my budget the ability to pay someone substantially more than all the rest. How do we pay for this additional expense?"

Good question. Glad you asked. Please suspend judgment for a few minutes until you get through the following paragraphs. Revolutionary change also requires radical thinking. Get ready for this ride right now.

I speak with supervisors, as well as with the employees, they designate as their "super performers." You'll notice, too, I didn't say "top performer." Even in a pool of mediocrity, you'll have a bell-shaped curve and someone who is the least mediocre will stand head and shoulders above the others.

That's part of why I'm not advocating hiring "the most qualified." The "most qualified" in a pool of mediocrity may simply be the least most mediocre person of the bunch. Try not to fall into this trap. Repost, re-recruit, re-start this process. Don't settle for the least most mediocre.

You'll be far, far ahead in the long run if you wait until you find the right person, that gem, the exceptional performer.

Then all you'll have to do is train them right, pay them right and treat them right. Hmm...well, some should probably just go ahead and hire the least most mediocre.

Every single one of the supervisors who I talked with said something like the following regarding their exceptional employee: "I don't have to supervise her." "He works circles around everyone else." "He produces three times as much as my other employees." (NOTE: as you've read, that number went up to seven as in "She produces I bet seven times as much as my other employees.") "I can't live without her."

☆☆☆☆☆ _____
☆☆☆☆☆ _____
☆☆☆☆☆ _____
☆☆☆☆☆ _____
☆☆☆☆☆ _____
☆☆☆☆☆ _____
☆☆☆☆☆ _____

And I created my preceding Model analyzing Tellers for a bank. With Tellers understanding who did the most transactions was easy because the bank's equipment tracks this…and, the bank's equipment told me that the least amount MORE than other "average" Tellers were doing was 4 times the amount and the most was 7 times.

So if Donnie, my "meets standards" Teller was doing 10 transactions an hour, Jane, my most exceptional, would be doing 70 transactions per hour and what was most interesting is customers preferred Jane, so she wasn't simply spinning through customers quickly; she was still building relationships.

Since very few people reading this are probably in banking I can use some real numbers (that may not make a lot of sense to those outside of banking), which I've rounded and made manageable, so they have a little "pretend" in them. And markets are different. What works in rural West Texas may not be the number in Houston (in fact I know it's not), but follow my logic for a minute and then I'll sum it all up. And those of you outside banking, if you hang in there for a few minutes, I think you can see the concept and formulas are most applicable to your business. If you can't get there, contact me and I'll try to help.

I'm going to show you how, but please understand the following numbers may or may not work based primarily on your technology. Our Tellers after our acquisition and with the introduction of antique technology would struggle to produce 2,500 transactions per month (our former standard).

I'm also using a base of $22,000 for a Teller and in Atlanta maybe this number is $28,000 and in New York maybe the number is $37,500 and in Duluth maybe the number is $26,000. I simply don't know.

Just increase or decrease the base to fit your market and realize the formula I share with you in the following will work for any position; you just may have to reset the base.

Let's say you manage a bank branch. You know, because "Corporate" has told you, an average Teller (cashing checks, doing a money order, analyzing an overdraft) can process 83.33 transactions a day, 10.42 per hour (those are real numbers and real standards we used).

You also know, as it's in your P&L report that your 8 Tellers make an average of $22,000 a year, $10.58 an hour. And in another report you've found that benefits (time off, health, dental, 401[k]) are adding another 30%, $6,600, to that base of $22,000.

So each Teller you have at your branch is costing you an average of $28,600 per year. Your lowest paid Teller makes $9.75 an hour; your highest makes $12.17 an hour. The spread between your highest paid Teller and your lowest is $2.42 an hour or $5,034 per year.

You're looking at all that data and thinking "that's pretty good."

Problem is, Bob, your lowest paid Teller, you would just as soon get rid of. He's been with you for 16 months, but his transaction volume is 41, less than half what an average Teller can do in a normal day.

Gail, your highest paid Teller averages 85 transactions a day, not setting the world on fire, but she's been around since dirt and although her attitude is something just above "The Grinch before he met the little Who," most days she's here on time and doesn't bother you very much.

Your branch is averaging 861 transactions per day, just under 108 transactions per Teller. You know that fairly non-aggressive average from Corporate per Teller is 83.33 per day. You have 8 Tellers. Your branch should be able to easily accommodate 667 transactions (8 Tellers X 83.33 transactions) per day and yet your branch is doing 861 transactions in a day. How are you doing that?

You look at the transaction report and see everyone, except Bob, is at or just above average. Except for Bob who's below and except for Mary who is...who is...who is...is that a misprint?

Mary falls about in the middle of the compensation range for your 8 Tellers. She makes $10.15 an hour. But, based on Mary's transaction volume, Mary just runs circles around everyone else. You wish you had more like her. You don't even consider yourself having to supervise her. She's the one who always has a smile on her face and she's the one customers line up to see.

You've always thought of Mary as being able to produce several times as much as everyone else. Today you look at the transactions for the year and the averages for each Teller and the report confirms this assumption. You smile because you knew it before the report showed you.

☆ ☆ ☆ ☆ ☆
☆ ☆ ☆ ☆ ☆
☆ ☆ ☆ ☆ ☆
☆ ☆ ☆ ☆ ☆
☆ ☆ ☆ ☆ ☆
☆ ☆ ☆ ☆ ☆
☆ ☆ ☆ ☆ ☆
☆ ☆ ☆ ☆ ☆

Mary's closest competitor does 93 transactions per day. Mary does, and here's the number you were questioning as a misprint, 312 transactions per day. You don't know what you would do if you lost Mary. Some customers would undoubtedly follow her. Your current group obviously couldn't handle the volume. You wish you could pay her more, but you have a budget and…

Here's the solution. You don't need 8 Tellers. You need three Tellers just like Mary because Mary is the definition of an exceptional employee, a person who works at three or four times (or more) the rate of everyone else, you don't need to supervise, is almost always in a good mood—your Model tells you all this.

Getting from where you are to where you need to be is easy to accomplish, although the numbers make the calculation a little cumbersome. Hang with me.

Excluding benefits, you're paying your 8 Teller group $176,000 per year. Give Mary a $7.00 per hour raise ($17.10 an hour, $35,672 per year) and hire two more just like her (you'll be slightly over-staffed, based on your current volume [861] transactions per day, but why not [861 transactions divided by 312, Mary's volume equals 2.75 Tellers with Mary's capacity]).

You don't have to start them at $35,672. Start them at $32,000. Your total Teller payroll will now be $99,672; the bank saves $76,338 and you have 3 Marys, people you don't have to supervise, people who work circles around the rest of the bank, people who aren't going anywhere, people who are happy and cheerful.

☆ ☆ ☆ ☆ ☆
☆ ☆ ☆ ☆ ☆
☆ ☆ ☆ ☆ ☆
☆ ☆ ☆ ☆ ☆
☆ ☆ ☆ ☆ ☆
☆ ☆ ☆ ☆ ☆
☆ ☆ ☆ ☆ ☆

"But I have all these other Tellers." You have to manage this process correctly. You have to be able to run over-staffed for just a little bit because you can't have your other 7 Tellers walk out the door. This will be the sales job you have to promote and get senior management to buy-in to.

Immediately, hire another Mary and then interview and have another Mary sitting in the wings, waiting for the opportunity. He or she will wait. They're making $7 or $8 per hour less than what you're offering. You can also use this third Mary position as a "just in case" someone on the staff steps up.

Next, after insuring you've hired another Mary, announce to the group that Mary is doing about four times the number of transactions of the next closest person. Because of this you've made the decision to give her a $7.00 an hour raise because her results demonstrates she's worth it.

And, you've hired Randi and you've hired her at slightly below Mary because she has all the attributes to perform at that level and that's your expectation that she will. And, you're agreeable to paying anyone else in your group that can perform at Mary's level, but this offer is only good for the first person to reach that level of performance and only to the person who can bring an attitude very much similar to Mary's and Randi's to the group.

Anyone who cannot achieve these new goals before you hire someone who can achieve these results will be offered the bank's standard severance package unless their performance goes down or fails to improve and then we'll offer the standard severance package sooner. Immediately following this very public meeting offer the severance package to Bob and send him out the door.

And, a quick aside. You may be reading this and thinking I'm suggesting taking your top performer and declaring him or her your "Exceptional Employee" and giving him or her a 35% to 60% increase. If you're thinking this you are wrong. You may not have an Exceptional Employee in your work group; chances are you do not. If you do, you know exactly who I am talking about. If you've had one in the past, you're thinking about him or her in your head right now.

These people are exceptional. They set your world on fire in a good way. When they announce their husband has been transferred, their leaving takes your breath away.

When they tell you they're going back to school to be a nurse, you support them on the outside, but hope they're grades won't allow them to get in.

When they come and tell you their wife has gotten a promotion and your exceptional performer has decided to home school the kids, you want to print out articles of all the fathers who have tried this and gone stark raving mad.

These are your Exceptional Employees.

☆☆☆☆☆
☆☆☆☆☆
☆☆☆☆☆
☆☆☆☆☆
☆☆☆☆☆
☆☆☆☆☆
☆☆☆☆☆

And you're going to get pushback on this plan from everyone from your supervisor to HR. However, a couple of things.

You're simply changing the rules in your workplace. This is something companies do constantly. There's nothing illegal, immoral or unethical about it. It's called "good business."

And, this process, although very difficult on individuals and very personal to them, is simply a reduction in force, so HR should have limited problem with it, although they'll probably jump up and down about it for a bit because, by and large, that's what many HR people do. It's their job and they're darned good at it.

There's nothing illegal, immoral or unethical about this concept and your decision.

The criteria for staying in your workgroup is based exclusively on performance and anyone who can perform can stay. Bob can't because he's already demonstrated he can't even perform at the bare minimum now. You should be able to show your supervisor on a piece of paper how you're going to break even on the budget in 12 months and be ahead of budget by the personnel cost savings within 18 months.

You can show her all the softer dollars too, your time to do more productive junk, like generate more business, being the big one.

A caveat. As mentioned you have to know if your technology can support the increased volume. When our bank sold a decision was made to move our Tellers backward to an archaic Teller platform, what they use to process transactions. This archaic Teller platform was the one used by the dominant bank.

Using this antiquated system our exceptional Tellers couldn't reach 2,500 transactions a month with an assistant and four more hours in everyone's day. This is true of all industries. The speed of any system, any system, is dependent on the speed of its slowest component.

Computers and the internet are classic examples. Many do not remember the 300 BAUD (300 BAUD simply being the speed of the connection) modem, but it's where some of us started. We used to be amazed in the computer lab to watch each letter appear as though someone behind the screen were typing it and in four or five or ten minutes a half page of text would be displayed on this little green screen and we'd all smile at this magic.

Think of the difference today where you can often have almost instantaneous access to a webpage.

Hook up all the fastest equipment you can possibly find with the fastest Ethernet, optics, whatever. Use all the super-whiz-bang devices to connect to the Internet and have mind-stunningly fast webpage access. Then somehow, at the frontend of that chain of Ethernet, computer, Internet, hook up a 300 BAUD modem and see how fast your super-fast system runs. It'll run at 300 BAUD, provided of course you can get it to run at all with this albatross.

The speed of any system, any system, is dependent on the speed of its slowest component.

In regard to making the transition from your current workgroup to an exceptional performance workgroup, the only question remains "can you do it?" The safe bet in my experience is to answer that question "no," but I follow that with "but I think you can."

The process may take a bit longer than I describe in the preceding. You may need to hire your next Mary and then insure you've hired a Mary and not a Bob, but as soon as you know that you have, you need to execute the plan.

You're biggest pushback is going to be senior management and whoever oversees "the budget." You may have to put your neck on the line, so make sure you're up to being a hero and not just up to being heroic.

Once started, you can't go back. You can't stop the plan's execution. You're being watched. Closely. Long-term career growth for yourself will not happen if you end up running a mediocre, over-staffed work group with the highest payroll expense by far in the company.

Do not…DO NOT…go into this thing halfway; you have to jump in with everything. This process takes someone who is not averse to extreme risk and there's always this fine line between risk and stupidity. You have to decide if you can withstand the withering pressure because for more time than is comfortable you're going to be looked on as being on the wrong side of that risk/stupidity line.

☆ ☆ ☆ ☆ ☆
☆ ☆ ☆ ☆ ☆
☆ ☆ ☆ ☆ ☆
☆ ☆ ☆ ☆ ☆
☆ ☆ ☆ ☆ ☆
☆ ☆ ☆ ☆ ☆
☆ ☆ ☆ ☆ ☆
☆ ☆ ☆ ☆ ☆

My advice in this regard would be to get as many senior managers to buy into the concept as you possibly can and experiment, understanding two things:

- first, the more people you include in the initial discussions the further public the intent of your actions become and your workgroup will find out from one of those "knights on a white horses" we have to deal with who are "fixing things," and
- second, the buck stops with you. Always.

There may be a concern of "well, what happens if all the other Tellers start performing at Mary's level." Here's the deal. None will.

That said, excluding Bob because he needs to be gone, you're going to be processing 2,184 transactions per day, if all 7 tellers are performing at Mary's level. You're either not going to have the business to justify 7 Tellers who can process this many transactions, at which point you offer severance to the lowest performers, or you're going to have the folks from Corporate in to see what the heck you're doing because they want to replicate whatever it is.

But dimes to donuts not a single existing employee will step up and the longer term employees will be the most difficult to get to move. Why?

Because we are who we are. I've used the old adage, "The best predictor of future performance is past performance" and you've probably read it about a zillion times outside of my work. Well, on the zillion and one time believe it as it's true.

The performance of your work group is the performance of each individual within that work group plus any synergy you've created. You can spend a fortune on training and consultants, but the needle isn't going to move a great, great deal, probably. My advice is to get your severance packages ready and start passing them out on day one.
"Bye, Bob. Take care."

And…AND…I'm not trying to be flipped or cruel. Bob is undoubtedly an exceptional person, may have family and financial obligations, so we must…MUST…treat him with absolute respect and treat him as right as we can in a very challenging and difficult relationship.

You'll have to pay your exceptional performers to keep them. If you don't, they have options. You have to pay them a lot more than the employees down the performance ladder. The only way you can do that is to increase your income or reduce your expenses.

Increasing your income is going to be very difficult because you're existing Teller group is only going to process so much and generate only so much income. That's true of every single work group in any industry anywhere. So you have to work on the expense side of the balance sheet.

Although I disagree with the concept that employees are an expense, they are if they're not producing what you need, and our jobs as managers and leaders is to ensure this expense is minimized.

You'll be producing more and spending less. You're branch will be brighter, happier, faster, more efficient. You'll have eliminated your turnover, which I won't go into the statistics, but is costing you a bundle. You won't be spending your days supervising/babysitting your staff and so you'll be out selling or procuring loans, or setting up business accounts, or…

The downside to this process is you'll have to have one difficult meeting, manage a difficult few weeks and have some difficult conversations with folks you've known for a bit and undoubtedly care about a lot. And you'll have to be the one, not HR (HR will guide you, but please hesitate using one of those gosh-awful HR-scripted, static and uncaring conversations—approach these conversations as a fellow human), who eliminates their positions and accepts this responsibility.

There's always some pain associated with a radically different approach. This is the "some pain," and it's admittedly substantial pain, of this modeling approach.

I know, too, there'll be those who will plan to accomplish what I'm suggesting through natural attrition. The problem with this scenario, besides the fact it won't work, is several-fold.

First, each and every year when you're doing annual increases you're going to have the painful conversations with all the other staff because you cannot pay them more for sitting there for another year.

Second, you're not going to be able to pay Mary the $7 an hour more and she's going to leave on you because some other company will pay her significantly more and $0.50 or $0.75 an hour more isn't going to hold her.

☆ ☆ ☆ ☆ ☆
☆ ☆ ☆ ☆ ☆
☆ ☆ ☆ ☆ ☆
☆ ☆ ☆ ☆ ☆
☆ ☆ ☆ ☆ ☆
☆ ☆ ☆ ☆ ☆
☆ ☆ ☆ ☆ ☆

Third, why are any of your existing folks going to leave? They're obviously comfortable doing what they're doing and now they can sit around and grumble and make your life even less enjoyable, and, yes, someone somewhere may offer them a little bit more, but, then, there's nothing "leadership" about hanging around and waiting for events to overtake you.

Fourth, if you have a plan and execute the plan, you can staff your organization appropriately. If you do not, then you're at the mercy of others making the decisions for you.

Fifth, the company isn't sitting still. They're wanting more and more from you each year. How do you intend to get there with staff that can't take you there? Who gets the severance package then?

Sixth, how the hell do we justify Mary's performance and pay to her or to ourselves? It's outrageously unfair. Sixth…Seventh…Eighth…

Not to repeat myself, but

The downside to this process is you'll have to have one difficult meeting, manage a difficult few weeks and have some difficult conversations with folks you've known for a bit and undoubtedly care about when you eliminate their positions.

There's always some pain associated with a radically different approach. This is the "some pain," and it's admittedly substantial pain.

☆ ☆ ☆ ☆ ☆
☆ ☆ ☆ ☆ ☆
☆ ☆ ☆ ☆ ☆
☆ ☆ ☆ ☆ ☆
☆ ☆ ☆ ☆ ☆
☆ ☆ ☆ ☆ ☆
☆ ☆ ☆ ☆ ☆
☆ ☆ ☆ ☆ ☆

You can more than offset the additional compensation in two areas: (1) increased production and (2) decrease headcount necessary to perform the same job.

Get out a sheet of paper and list the downside to the preceding.

I am concerned, but not overly concerned, about what "our existing" employees will say or think. If they're of this "exceptional" caliber they should be compensated accordingly as well, and, if they're not, they shouldn't be. We should be able to demonstrate to existing employees what we require to get to this next level and then we should be able to measure if and when they get there.

I've held these sorts of conversations with staff and I've experienced the incredible turnover briefly, so in the words of President Bill Clinton, "I feel your pain." The other side of this however is that the new workplace is definitely worth the pain and the productivity is definitely worth the pain.

Scientifically validated studies indicate an "exceptional performer" has the capacity to produce up to 2,000% (yes, 2,000) above an "average performer." I do not have an idea of how "they" (the researchers) arrive at that 2,000% number.

A scientific study to me, where as many variables as are reasonable are eliminated, carries with it some pretty significant validity. And, even if the number is 250%, I think that sort of productivity is worth supporting. 2000% percent, of the 83 transactions per day average, in my example in the preceding, is 1,667 transactions per day. In the preceding example your branch is only doing 861 transactions per day. To cover this volume, you need to hire one of these exceptional employees and have them work part-time.

In this regard, we should be willing to reward this sort of effort and reward this effort handsomely. And, we should be willing then to look at our staffing as a legitimate way to pay for this new system. If we are unwilling to look at our staffing levels in the context of our employee group's productivity, then we should be unwilling to look at increasing our rewards to our Exceptional Employees. One does not fly without the other.

And, if we cannot consider the preceding, we should live with what we have as, unless the organization is willing to absorb some significantly higher compensation costs, we cannot move forward with the plan I propose. But the preceding takes leadership. Any leaders out there?

On Interviewing and Taking Notes

When you sit to perform an interview please consider having another manager or senior employee with you. This person can either be another note taker or can be a questioner and note taker. The more copious your note taking, in the right way, the better your ending evaluation will be.

Tell the candidate that you are going to be scribbling notes and you're not ignoring him or her or attempting to be discourteous, but you want to make sure you have sufficient information to make a good decision. (I usually bring a laptop and take notes on this, but, then, if I don't I

☆ ☆ ☆ ☆ ☆
☆ ☆ ☆ ☆ ☆
☆ ☆ ☆ ☆ ☆
☆ ☆ ☆ ☆ ☆
☆ ☆ ☆ ☆ ☆
☆ ☆ ☆ ☆ ☆
☆ ☆ ☆ ☆ ☆
☆ ☆ ☆ ☆ ☆

often can't read most of my scribbling and my hand gets real tired, so, without a laptop, I quit taking real good notes about half way through an interview, which is not a desired outcome.)

Immediately following the interview, take 10–15 minutes to read over your notes and add and delete as you see a need (you should not be discussing the candidate at this point with the other note taker, but he or she probably should be involved in the same exercise of rereading their notes).

Remember, too, you're looking for notes that will aid you in evaluating the candidate against your Model, so you may want to read over your Model real quickly before sitting down to this task. Even if you've used your Model document as your foundation and simply jotted notes in the margins, read over it again and then read over your notes.

And, if you didn't find the candidate worth the interview, don't spend any more time on this process. I'm a firm believer in stopping the process when you know there's not a fit.

There are some legal liabilities associated with this, like if all the black candidates get short interviews, or the person in the wheelchair hardly gets past the first question. But you should have a very legitimate reason for stopping the interview. "I was tired" won't work. "We needed a relationship builder and John could only share with us relationships he'd mangled and we gave him multiple opportunities, but he didn't come up with any positive examples." There's a legitimate reason to cut an interview short.

☆☆☆☆☆ _____
☆☆☆☆☆ _____
☆☆☆☆☆ _____
☆☆☆☆☆ _____
☆☆☆☆☆ _____
☆☆☆☆☆ _____
☆☆☆☆☆ _____

What we've seemed to have done in the past few years is build all our processes, policies and procedures to avoid the boogeyman of litigation. I'd like to propose we be careful, but refocus on our businesses and there's nothing quite as critical as finding the right people to do the right job.

We may have difficulty successfully exercising this goal if we can't exorcise the boogeyman of litigation from our every thought process. And here's an idea, if you have an HR person who simply uses the "we'll get sued" excuse every time someone brings up anything even minimally controversial, it's time for a new HR person. With some pretty minimal effort the chances of a company being involved in employment litigation are pretty small (this may change rather perpetually, and I'm not saying it should or shouldn't, with a change in presidents and/or parties) and if an HR person cannot give you the specific reasons behind his "because we'll get sued" he's the wrong person for this vital role.

Asking behavioral questions will seem awkward at first. "Describe for me…" or "Tell me about…" are not the most natural ways we usually ask questions. Most these sorts of queries don't even end with question marks.

You'll find candidates really struggle sometimes with what you're asking for. You really need to consider taking a few minutes and sitting down with your Model and your questions and attempting to insure you know before the interview what answers would most meet your requirements.

As you keep using this process, it will pay huge dividends, but you cannot expect to be proficient at anything by doing some "thing" a couple of times.

With this process, based on a Model, you're probably going to do a much better job of hiring a better candidate right off the bat than you've been doing with a traditional interview, but just guessing, even with my work, you're probably six or eight or ten hiring decisions away from having that light bulb come on in your head and experiencing an "ah ha!" moment and selecting an exceptional performer.

Don't give up on the process. After each hiring decision take just a few minutes and think about things you'll do differently next time. Try keeping a legal pad of these "jotted suggestions to self." You'll like the outcome in just a little bit of time.

Generally, start to finish, you spend 75–90 minutes, maybe a couple of hours for a really long one, in the interview and reviewing and editing your notes. This may seem like a lot of time, but in the overall scheme of an exceptional employee's career, finding a better expenditure of your time would be difficult. Think of a poor hiring decision you, or someone you know has made; how much time did he or she spend dealing with the nonsense? As Charles "Red" Scott of Pier One Imports said "You can never pay the right person enough, and you always pay the wrong person too much—no matter what the number." This process is designed to select the right person. It will require an investment, however.

☆ ☆ ☆ ☆ ☆
☆ ☆ ☆ ☆ ☆
☆ ☆ ☆ ☆ ☆
☆ ☆ ☆ ☆ ☆
☆ ☆ ☆ ☆ ☆
☆ ☆ ☆ ☆ ☆
☆ ☆ ☆ ☆ ☆

At the end of the interview your goal is very simple. You must be able to compare a candidate's responses to your Model. If you're able to do this, you will have a much higher degree of success in predicting whether the person you're considering hiring will potentially be an exceptional performer. The closer someone aligns with your Model, the closer you are to hiring that elusive exceptional performer.

And I think if I see one mistake more than any other in this deal it is in the taking of copious notes. Your goal, again, is not to jot down everything coming out of someone's mouth.

Your goal is to align what the person is saying to your Model. This can be as easy as underlining the critical elements of your Model, "great relationship builder," and jotting a "YES!!!" in the margins. I wouldn't advocate simply jotting a "YES!!!" as it really doesn't say much and you do want to be able to rebuild the interview from your notes in case you are ever asked, but you can jot "YES!!!

See explanation on notes #3" where your "notes #3" is a legal pad or a laptop and #3 gives a more detailed description of what brought you to "YES!!!" Remember, this is your interview. If you have to take a few minutes to jot some notes, the interviewee will gladly wait. And sometimes the extra silence pays dividends.

After the interviews are done, you're going to be left with a stack of notes on each candidate. You're going to be able to eliminate several very quickly. They're going to have a few of the skills, attributes and behaviors you're looking for, but they're also going to be lacking in a couple of areas (and, remember, these are the areas you defined as part of the exceptional performer's package). Someone missing a skill or talent in a normal interview may not be cause for enormous worry. Someone missing the same skill or especially talent (as a skill is generally trainable and a talent not so much) here probably excludes themselves. And then you'll just have to decide how closely you need the person sitting in front of you to align with your Model. I'd recommend "pretty darn close" as a little difference makes a lot of difference, but "pretty darn close" is something you'll have to decide on and it will become more clear as you get into The Model, the interviews and note taking.

The Next Most Difficult Question

Let me explain a problem with this whole Model thing and a potential problem with the preceding plan regarding compensation. Let me put this as the very last thing in this manuscript because it is the most important concept I think I came up with and it's pretty simple: The next most difficult question.

As you traverse the Model I built specifically for Tellers, but one where many of the queries can be used for any customer-facing positions, so long as they answer questions related to the picture your Model has drawn for you, you'll notice me saying things like "ask the next most difficult question," or recommending a "follow-up."

Let me try to explain what I mean. I have numerous follow-up suggestions in my Model questions that I've shared with managers and have given you here as examples, but follow-ups are very tricky. I'm not going to be sitting in the room (probably) during the conversation you have with your candidate and I can't whisper "ask this question." So, you can read my work, use it to develop your Model, use it to put together a host of incredible questions, but then you're on your own. That's sort of the way this process works. Sooner or later momma bird is going to kick you out of the nest and you're going to have to fly. Now seems about as good a time as any.

I'd advocate that you think deeply about what you're asking and what answer you're seeking. This will lead you to the next most difficult question, the follow-up when the candidate invariably goes off on a bunny trail and you're no closer to the answer you needed than when you started.

Let me also let you know something sort of depressing right here. I advocated earlier you have another person in the room. For the first few years I was messing with this "behavioral" stuff I'd explain to the candidate that the other person who was in the room would be asking the questions and I would be typing furiously on my laptop to try and collect as much information as I possibly could and to please simply ignore my flying hands and ignore the fact that I wasn't going to be interacting and ignore the fact that sometimes I'd be typing like a possessed maniac and other times I'd appear to be completely disengaged. My job in this process was listening intently and recording accurately everything the interviewee was saying.

I did this for several years because I'm not that bright.

It took me that long, and again as I explained in the interviewing section in the preceding, to realize what is wrong with behavior-based

☆ ☆ ☆ ☆ ☆
☆ ☆ ☆ ☆ ☆
☆ ☆ ☆ ☆ ☆
☆ ☆ ☆ ☆ ☆
☆ ☆ ☆ ☆ ☆
☆ ☆ ☆ ☆ ☆
☆ ☆ ☆ ☆ ☆
☆ ☆ ☆ ☆ ☆

interviewing. Behavior-based interviewing is better than the usual fly by the seat of your pants interview where someone asks a bunch of irrelevant, and/or inane questions and then everyone shakes hands and this interviewer repeats this process and then usually hires the last one interviewed because the interviewer can't really remember the others all that well and is tired and ready to be done. Behavior-based interviewing is a lot better than this sort of process, but the problem with behavior-based interviewing is when you get done you have an absolutely accurate record of the interview. Lawyers, generally, love this process because of its attention to detail and I'm not saying all this detail is wrong. It simply isn't always what you need.

When you go back to your copious notes, you find you've recorded a sterile description of the interview that just took place, but you're probably no closer to a legitimate decision than you were before you started. And maybe there's a matrix HR has developed associated with your behavioral interview and you've checked "meets criteria" more often than you've checked "hasn't the foggiest idea what I'm talking about." And you add up all those checks for each candidate and one person has six positives, and one has nine and one has eleven and one has ten and one has seven and another has nine and you hire the one with eleven and the one with seven was actually the person you liked the best, but you can't put your finger on why.

But the process said "eleven."

You have scientifically, mechanically selected the person your process has told you most meets the criteria you defined on your job description and laid out neatly on the matrix and all the lawyers in the room are happier than Betty getting a date with Archie over Veronica. I've always wondered what's the big deal with Archie, but that's probably a topic for another time.

And the preceding process is much, much, much better than the process you have used in the past and you still didn't hire who it is you needed to hire. Probably.

To some degree the process of our Model fixes this, but to some degree it does not. I can almost guarantee you that you're going to do your first interviews using your Model and when you get done you're going to wonder what you have and it will turn out you don't have what you need, but you have very copious notes. You may even develop a post-interview matrix and go back to your notes and try to complete the matrix.

Your Model isn't the problem. It's so far superior to a job description as to be comparing an ox-drawn cart to a drone delivery system.

You may follow this copious note process, however (maybe even, hope not, for a couple of years, if you have that kind of persistence), and then a little bell will ding in your head, a light bulb will click on, or some other appropriate analogy will appear and you'll get it.

What you'll get is an understanding that simply taking copious notes, recording your conversations with a candidate isn't ever going to yield you more than you were given during the interview. You're not actively listening; you're actively recording. This isn't the worst thing you could do, but it doesn't get you to your Model.

A simple example. One of sort of a second tier attribute I found when I built my Model for an exceptional Teller was that this group of employees tended to smile a lot.

I could go through an entire interview process with multiple candidates and write down every single word each and every one said and when I got done I would be no closer to knowing whether this group of candidates had this primary, albeit second tier, attribute I was looking for.

I wouldn't know this unless I knew exactly what I was looking for and I wrote in my notes "this person appears to smile a lot," and/or "this person smiles frequently and with relative ease. Very comfortable person." Or, I could go overboard and have a "Smile Scorecard" and every time the person smiled I could check a box and at the end of the process add up the smiles and hire the "eleven," but this "Smile Scorecard" is not what I'm trying to accomplish with this process. I want to observe a relaxed, engaged, dare I say happy person and checkmarks and copious notes don't get me to that definition.

There are several keys to understanding the difference and I know most are looking at the preceding and thinking "well, duh," but it's a deeper understanding than "well, duh."

First, you have to know your Model you build inside and out, what you're looking for. Job descriptions give you specific tasks and you go through and ask someone "can you pick up a wrench, crawl under the sink, fiddle around under there all the while showing the appropriate level of butt crack?" The question may not be that straightforward and

☆ ☆ ☆ ☆ ☆
☆ ☆ ☆ ☆ ☆
☆ ☆ ☆ ☆ ☆
☆ ☆ ☆ ☆ ☆
☆ ☆ ☆ ☆ ☆
☆ ☆ ☆ ☆ ☆
☆ ☆ ☆ ☆ ☆

the answer certainly will not be, but there's a list of tasks that someone has to be able to perform to align with the details on the job description.

You're functioning with a job description in a single dimension.

Your Model is a composite picture of the person who could best perform the job. You're functioning, now, in multi-dimensions. Going into the interview you have to have that picture burned in your head and as the candidate talks you're not writing down verbatim everything he or she says, you're jotting notes about how he or she aligns to your Model—How he or she aligns to your Model.

Please stop, go back and reread that last sentence in that last paragraph again.

Okay, now reread that last line about seventeen times right now and then reread it again about twenty times before each interview.

If you take copious notes during an interview and the interview lasts for an hour, you will have six or seven typed, single-spaced pages of notes. If you follow the preceding advice—related to aligning your interview to your Model—you might get to a single page or maybe a couple of pages of notes.

The difference is your single page of notes will give you a comparison to your Model, but the six or seven typed, single-spaced pages of notes may not. The difference, too, is you'll be a lot less tired with one page of notes, but that's not really a good reason for doing anything.

As I've alluded to you can print your Model on a sheet of paper in front of you and have enough room in the margins and draw little arrows to the attributes you're looking for and say things like "Yep, her story about the customer who was irate because she purchased a puppy that wets on the rug demonstrated she understands the steps of problem solving. Think she might fit in here, if she can get rid of the dog she took off the customer's hands."

However, getting to the point where you can make that note isn't as easy as simply flipping to some of the questions I have throughout the preceding Model chapter and saying "this one looks close enough." Instead you have to continue to dig until you get to the answer. I call the process of drilling down, digging for the answer, the next most difficult question.

I'll use a simple example. Usually you can glean from an application whether someone has the requisite experience in terms of education and/or computer-type experience. However, I'm kind of a computer buff and really like what the software can do and really honor someone who has this skill set. Plus these folks can get a heck-uv-a-lot more done, generally speaking, using technology than can some who do not understand this tool. The following is an actual conversation I had with someone interviewing for a benefits position.

Me: Tell me about the most involved spreadsheet you ever built and how you went about building this and any obstacles you had to overcome.

Him: We had this project where we needed to track when people would change into a new five-year age bracket. This was for life-insurance purposes and so we needed to know when someone would move from say the 30-plus age group to the 35-plus age group because as you know this negatively impacts someone in terms of how much he or she has to pay for the same amount of coverage. So that's what this spreadsheet did. We'd simply have to key in the new rates at the beginning of the year and the spreadsheet would calculate the amount of benefit and the cost to the user based on their age and the coverages he or she selected. The sheet had multiple files that it would pull relevant table information from, so after we completed it, all we had to do was to periodically go in and update these tables. We had several technical problems that we had to work through and our manager was pretty much on us in terms of getting this thing completed, so those are the obstacles we had to overcome to get this thing done. When all was said and done, however, this deal was way cool and really fun to work with.

If you know Excel, you know the preceding is a fairly complex pseudo-database type problem that probably uses "V" or "H" look-up tables or more probably uses a pivot table. All of these things are a few steps above the level of understanding necessary to do things like add a column of numbers. So, there was definitely some advanced understanding of Excel indicated, but did he answer my query: "Tell me about the most involved spreadsheet you ever built and how you went about building this and any obstacles you had to overcome?"

Think about this "did he answer my question" for a second because this is real critical to understanding this idea of a Model and the next most difficult question. My Model called for someone with some pretty decent understanding of Excel and the ability to work within this rather amazing software to make some interesting things happen. Did this candidate's response answer this question for me?

Asked another way "Did this candidate build this spreadsheet?"

By his response I couldn't tell. This is the value of this process and thinking about the answer and not simply recording a response. I know what I'm looking for and he may not, although I'm not averse to sharing a Model and my queries with the candidate and in fact doing this poses some interesting advantages.

I'm still the one who is going to be analyzing what is said and comparing this person to my work group and culture and although the person could probably glean things like "smiles a lot" and try to improve in these sorts of categories, I haven't found anyone yet who has "fooled my Model," or the process, or they've fooled me so well that I can't tell the difference.

However, after all the long response in which the candidate is thinking "I've answered the question," I have to be willing to ask the next most difficult question. I refer to the next most difficult question by this title because as we probe further into the person's answers we're basically

☆ ☆ ☆ ☆ ☆
☆ ☆ ☆ ☆ ☆
☆ ☆ ☆ ☆ ☆
☆ ☆ ☆ ☆ ☆
☆ ☆ ☆ ☆ ☆
☆ ☆ ☆ ☆ ☆
☆ ☆ ☆ ☆ ☆

having to say "no, that didn't answer my question," or "okay, that was a nice snow job; let's go after the truth this time."

Here's how the conversation progressed.

Me: Wow, that sounds like an incredible spreadsheet.

Him: It was real complicated, but once finished, worked like a champ.

Me: Tell me how you got the software to analyze the correlation between age and policy to the extent that you were able to simply type in the new rates and the software then would calculate the premium.

Him: What?

Me: [I repeated the query], but I knew the snow wasn't falling quite as hard in my office at the moment and the snow job was ending as the light of a new spring was dawning.

Him: Well, I'd simply type in the new rates in a table and then open the primary source document and look for any of the appropriately aged employees we had who had moved into a new age category and where the row and column intersected the new premium rate would be displayed broken down by bi-weekly payroll, weekly, monthly and then on an annualized basis.

When the words start getting bigger and the sentences start getting more convoluted you should dial your "nonsense" meter to "HIGH" and start seeking the answer behind the snow. If you read his preceding response out loud, it's almost laughable. What it says is he's typing in numbers in a table and then Excel is calculating new amounts. This is basic data entry.

Me: Okay, that gives me some good information, but what formulas did you use to get the sheet to calculate the amounts displayed where the row and the column intersected.

Him: There were numerous formulas that we used to get to that calculation. We had multiple spreadsheets and numerous tables and each was tied to one another. If you opened a spreadsheet and it was tied to another Excel always asked "do you want to update such and such sheet" and you'd always have to respond and click the "OK" button.

I won't belabor this conversation further, but the point is if I had been simply recording the answers he was giving me I probably would have stopped with the first query and said "good enough." And maybe checked the box on the matrix under "Excel knowledge" "meets criteria."

But I had my Model in front of me and the picture I was attempting to get to was of someone who had some pretty advanced knowledge of Excel. What I also hadn't heard yet was "I." I kept getting "we." By using "we" he wasn't lying to me, but he wasn't being completely honest either. I eventually had to ask the following and I received the following reply:

☆ ☆ ☆ ☆ ☆
☆ ☆ ☆ ☆ ☆
☆ ☆ ☆ ☆ ☆
☆ ☆ ☆ ☆ ☆
☆ ☆ ☆ ☆ ☆
☆ ☆ ☆ ☆ ☆
☆ ☆ ☆ ☆ ☆

Me: Okay, no more "we." I want you to start the next answer with "I" as in "I did" and then complete the thought. Tell me specifically using a specific example of a formula you built that became part of this spreadsheet.

Him: Well, as I said, I'd open the spreadshe…"

Me: Start with "I" as in "I did," or "I wrote," or "I built."

There was a dead space. He sat there and I sat there. It was uncomfortably quiet.

Him: What I did was open the spreadsheet and type in the new rates and the spreadsheet gave me the numbers.

He did data entry. The snow was no longer falling. Spring had sprung, not in his world, but in mine. That was the extent of his knowledge of Excel. Without the next most difficult question(s), without continuous follow-up, I wouldn't have gotten to that level of understanding.

I'm not sure if I would have hired this person, but I definitely did not and that "definitely" was built on a substantial missing skill set that my exceptional performer owned.

This understanding of Excel was one of my core requirements of this Model. It was a skill set the person coming in had to have. If he or she did not, I was prepared to keep looking. This candidate did not have this skill and I thanked him for his time and the interview ended ten or fifteen minutes after it had begun. We never got past the first query and that was fine.

Some may view the preceding as sort of mean, kind of unfriendly, not very nice, too tough. My future and the company's future is dependent on the people I hire. Call it "lying," or "coloring the truth," or "embellishing," or "misspeaking," but I only ask the questions and ask for an honest response. When I don't get it,

I owe it to myself and to the company to keep digging until I have the answer I need to make the best decision be that a negative consequence or a positive one for my interviewee.

The person I eventually hired, after reposting the position…twice… had the prerequisite skill, so there was no liability in not hiring the person without the prerequisite skill. Imagine sitting after five or six or more interviews and looking through page after page of notes trying to discern who did and who did not meet my basic requirements. I possibly would have never chosen the Exceptional Performer.

I give you all this detail, all this information so that you don't have to beat your head against my wall. I spent the first four or five years of my career trying to figure out interviewing and then ran into behavior-based interviewing.

I spent the next two or three years trying to figure that process out and wondering why I couldn't make better hiring decision using this technique, although in retrospect I was at the advertised 55%. I spent the next couple of years messing around with all sorts of progressively more complicated scoring matrices, jotting notes and experimenting.

Then I started focusing on building the composite sketch of someone really performing a job at a phenomenal level—the best of the best of the best.

And I messed around with matrices and questions and note taking techniques and I finally ended up with my one or two page Model sitting on the table in front of me, my list of ten or maybe fifteen questions and a pen. That's all you need:

An absolutely well-defined Model;

A great understanding of that Model;

A printed copy of your Model with plenty of room in the margins or an additional blank sheet(s) of paper;

A pen;

Some really good listening skills;

The guts to ask and continue to ask the next most difficult question.

Since, I've perfected my Model, I have made exceptional hiring decisions (knock on wood). Before then, I struggled to make a good one. And that brings me to my final two points.

The process of hiring usually functions as a process of exclusion rather than inclusion. In the traditional setting and using a traditional hiring process we look at a stack of applications and resumes and we begin picking through them anxious to whittle the stack down to a manageable number. To do this we're looking for reasons to exclude people: sloppy, gaps in employment, incomplete history, no 10-key skills, not a high school graduate, misspellings and poor grammar, not signed, no date, just doesn't look like someone I'm interested in, etc., etc., etc.

Then we move on to the interviews. We may have gleaned from a stack of 30 or 60 or 90 or 120, two or three or four or five folks we want to interview. We sit down and we ask them a series of questions all the while trying to figure out ways to get from five to one.

And maybe we're looking to replace a salesperson and so when quiet and reserved Angela sits down in front of us we know immediately she isn't it, but to appease that "darned human resources department" we go ahead and go through all the questions and surprisingly she does pretty good, but she's just too "mousey" and we go on to the next person and he's got a tattoo on the back of his hand and "who puts a tattoo on the back of their hand" and "how can you meet the public with such a thing" and so again to appease that "darned HR group" we go through the questions, but he was eliminated at the handshake.

And so the process continues with us looking for reasons to not hire someone.

☆ ☆ ☆ ☆ ☆
☆ ☆ ☆ ☆ ☆
☆ ☆ ☆ ☆ ☆
☆ ☆ ☆ ☆ ☆
☆ ☆ ☆ ☆ ☆
☆ ☆ ☆ ☆ ☆
☆ ☆ ☆ ☆ ☆

When we get done with our five interviews we have the five bloody corpses laying in front of us and "is this really the best we can do?" and then we see one of the corpses sort of flinch and we think "hey, that's impressive. She survived this grueling process. She has spunk. Salespeople need spunk. Salespeople need to be survivors."

And so we make our decision and maybe it works out and even if she's not exactly going great guns, we're not paying her that much and she's on commission anyway and "okay, she sort of goes overboard on the perfume, but that's not a reason to fire someone" and we build our team.

The process used by many is one of exclusion rather than inclusion.

With our Model we're on a quest and it's a noble quest. We're looking for someone who is absolutely going to blow everyone away and make our lives dramatically easier. We're looking to include as many folks as is necessary to find not the "most qualified," but the person who absolutely, positively fits our Model, or comes awful gosh-darned close…with potential. The whole paradigm of our Model is different than the usual hiring process.

So please understand your Model is a process of inclusion not exclusion. Also, please understand even someone like me, who spent a couple of decades building this process and worked with it across multiple industries, sometimes makes a really bad decision. Nothing is perfect.

☆ ☆ ☆ ☆ ☆
☆ ☆ ☆ ☆ ☆
☆ ☆ ☆ ☆ ☆
☆ ☆ ☆ ☆ ☆
☆ ☆ ☆ ☆ ☆
☆ ☆ ☆ ☆ ☆
☆ ☆ ☆ ☆ ☆
☆ ☆ ☆ ☆ ☆

Here's an example of my last imperfection, which really drove me to reanalyze what I consider to be my life's work and to perfect this whole hiring thing. And please note, I've changed a whole bunch of information regarding the following, including taking some liberties and using a composite, somewhat of a caricature of the people I've dealt with throughout their years, so there's really no way to figure out who it is I'm talking about.

The essence of the following, however, is true and it was the catalyst for me to try and come up with a method to insure I didn't make decisions like the following ever again. And, so far, knock on wood again, I have not.

I established a great behavior-based interviewing process, complete with a matrix and a questionnaire. The benefits position I was hiring for was in an area that was geographically removed and so having someone who could supervise himself or herself was paramount. I had a three page job description that boiled everything down to the very most basic tasks.

I posted the position and recruited heavily. I took my time, using a matrix to analyze resumes and applications. I didn't find anyone that jumped off the page, but I ended up with five folks to interview. I put a team together and for two days we went through each candidate. I had them all answer my questionnaire, which was benefits-related questions that a seasoned benefits person would know.

When we were done with the interviews my basic impression was "well, a couple were 'okay,'" but I didn't feel like I'd found the right person. The three managers I had asked to sit in on the interviews agreed and, although the position had now been open for 60 days and I was getting very tired, I reposted it at a higher compensation and waited. I had made the decision to interview candidates as they came in. The managers I had selected to help went back to their real jobs and so I'd interview the candidates alone. I also eliminated the questionnaire as I felt their application and resume should sufficiently answer the questions with the exception of the writing sample.

Bernie sent in his application and as I looked at it he seemed, and I hoped, he had the skills I needed. I set up an interview and it went okay. I asked another of the managers to talk with him for a moment and this manager said "he's okay; I don't think he's going to make anyone real happy, but he's better than the others." I agreed. I extended an offer and we messed around for a few days with little nonsensical things. Finally, Bernie said yes, with the caveat "but I have to have some time to close out all I have going on at the hospital as I just can't leave them hanging." I agreed and extended the start date out 30 days.

Bernie came on board and I was just happy to have a warm body in a chair. Bernie wanted to work on his master's degree and chose one of those ridiculously expensive and fairly worthless programs that dot the Internet. I was fine with all of it.

The company assisted where we could. Bernie kept asking me to look at the tuition reimbursement program and increase it. I kept saying "after you're done" would be a more appropriate time for HR to make this change since making the change now would positively impact one of our own and I felt would be perceived as favoritism and that's sort of the death knoll for HR. He was none too happy and next started advocating for progressively greater salary increases.

When he finished his degree he told me he wanted substantially more money. I told him the position paid what it paid and I had told him on the front-end of his tenure.

His behavior went from odd to bizarre and I finally received a call from his assistant he had demanded I hire. As I listened to him explain the circumstances and the increasingly bizarre behavior, I knew I had a bad apple, who was very dishonest, and knew I had to do something.

The end came when I made a surprise late week visit to Bernie's office, found it a wreck and found he hadn't even been to the office that week, answering emails remotely from home. He was out because of "stress," but he was so stressed out he hadn't bothered even to call. I sort of figured he was stressed because he wasn't doing anything, but not being a doctor I couldn't offer this diagnosis.

I fired Bernie and he filed unemployment. We initially won, but I didn't bother to fight the next level of unemployment as he had filed an EEOC complaint and I didn't want to give him ammunition or insight into our response to the EEO. We of course won the EEO as well as Bernie had no legitimate complaint, but Bernie received the usual and customary "Right to Sue" letter. And he did. We proceeded to mediation and settled for maybe a third of what I would have been willing to pay just to get rid of him. Unfortunately this system is also fairly screwed up. There's no liability or cost for the ex-employee and when you're dealing with a habitual liar like Bernie his case can be a bit of a minefield.

I have a habit of after a hire going back and analyzing what I did right and what I did wrong. With Bernie, who turned out to be a world class liar of the habitual type, I'd made several mistakes. First, I'd gotten way too tired doing Bernie's job and doing mine and got progressively more desperate.

Second, as the negotiations for his services stretched into the mundane, the little voice of discomfort I had from the outset started growing louder and louder and louder. I couldn't turn it off, but I also didn't listen to it. My gut was trying to warn me of impending trouble; my brain wouldn't listen. Bad decision.

Third, I made an error that I harp on with my managers not to make. I failed to check references. If I had I might have found that Bernie was on leave from the hospital. I don't know how much information I would have found out from the hospital, but if I could have gotten even a small sense that he wasn't there to go back and "finish up important things," I might have started listening to my gut. I failed to perform this basic step and I have made a point never, ever, never to do that again.

Fourth, early in his tenure there was trouble and I failed to address it adequately. Managers were perpetually upset with his response time and I was constantly having to referee. I manage my people a lot better now, but as soon as you know you've made a poor hiring decision, you need to step in and end it. The person that replaced Bernie turned out to be real, real regimented, which in benefits is fine, but she turned out to be real, real mean as well. I found out about this in the first month of employment and let her go. You cannot react too fast to a disastrous hiring decision. Remember, these first few months should be the best performance and behavior the person has to offer. I should have taken the opportunity early with Bernie and gotten him out of the organization.

Fifth, I didn't want to address Bernie's failings thinking a warm body was better than no body. I gave him decent performance appraisals and an annual increase. I would kick myself to this day if I believed in dwelling on past errors. I do not and I've not made that mistake again with anyone. My people get legitimate performance appraisals.

I should'a, could'a, would'a, but all we can do is learn from these pitiful wastes of resources and I learned plenty from Bernie, besides the fact he is lying scum that I would never wish on a future employer. For that what I ended up paying him, which was about what I offered him to quietly go away in the first place (less his attorney fees), was more than worth the experience and the learning experience. It taught me so much, but most importantly it taught me to really get this hiring junk down to a science, which is exactly what I did. Here's what I learned:

Build and follow a Model;

Ask behavioral questions;

Ask the next most difficult questions;

☆ ☆ ☆ ☆ ☆
☆ ☆ ☆ ☆ ☆
☆ ☆ ☆ ☆ ☆
☆ ☆ ☆ ☆ ☆
☆ ☆ ☆ ☆ ☆
☆ ☆ ☆ ☆ ☆
☆ ☆ ☆ ☆ ☆

1. Take the right notes;

2. Make sure you do extensive, extensive background checks. Talk with everyone you can possibly find to talk with (once you get two or three references [hopefully someone not on your candidate's list] saying the same thing, you have what you need to make a decision);

3. Check everything you possibly can: google.com is a great starting point, Facebook, LinkedIn, Instagram, Google+, YouTube, any of the other social networking sites are great. Do not stop until every single concern is allied;

4. Then, if the person you hired is not the person who comes to work, offer them a decent (a few weeks) going away package and get rid of them. If they don't accept the going away package or want to argue it, point out that this decision and package is not a negotiation.

5. You must be willing, too, to ask the next most difficult question. If someone fails to respond in a way where you can make an informed decision based on your Model, follow-up with a more pointed (not meaner, but more on point) question. This is probably the most difficult skill to develop in behavioral interviewing and definitely is key to getting your Model to work for you.

6. You will notice in the explanation and answers sections (the preceding chapter) of this document that I will say something like "this question may be incredibly difficult to answer." Use these questions as kind of the "separate the men (or women) from the boys (or girls)." If you have two candidates with similar qualifications, you may be able to

☆☆☆☆☆
☆☆☆☆☆
☆☆☆☆☆
☆☆☆☆☆
☆☆☆☆☆
☆☆☆☆☆
☆☆☆☆☆
☆☆☆☆☆

discriminate one from the other based on their response to one of these "super-tough" questions.

As you ask your questions, you may find you get an answer that covers one or two or more of your other questions. Reading the question to yourself and then simply telling the candidate, "I'm going to go ahead and skip this question because you seem to have answered it earlier" is most appropriate. Sometimes you can skip a single question without explanation, but if you end up in an interview and four of your ten questions are answered right off the bat, the length of the interview may shrink dramatically and require some explanation.

That's about all the advice I can give in this deal. Stick with your Model and I can guarantee you results. Keep tweaking what you're doing, constantly questioning your decisions, always looking for things that work and don't work.

As I mentioned earlier, I was asked by a really good friend one day, as he was starting his own business, "Rex, if you could give me one piece of over-arching HR advice, what would that be?" Here it is and I live by it:

Hire really smart, really happy people and pay them really well.

I know that doesn't exactly fit into this work on hiring, especially not just sort of stuck here, but that's the magic. You follow that single guideline and your workgroup will thrive. If your workgroup thrives, your business should grow.

☆☆☆☆☆
☆☆☆☆☆
☆☆☆☆☆
☆☆☆☆☆
☆☆☆☆☆
☆☆☆☆☆
☆☆☆☆☆

Finally, I used as my title *Selecting The Brass Ring*. When you ride one of the old, old merry-go-rounds, you reach out on your way past and try to snag the brass ring. You sort of lurch for it as your horse either is on an uptick or a downward slide. Sometimes you luck out and get the science right and you snatch the brass ring. You're not on a merry-go-round with your Model. You're sitting there looking at five, six or seven rings in front of you and when you get done with your interview, you're hopefully looking at one or two real shiny brass ones and if you're not, you make a decision whether to select five more and try again, or to pick one of the ones that maybe isn't as bright as you desire, but you can work on.

There's nothing merry-go-round about this process and your hiring decisions shouldn't make you dizzy. If they do, go back to your Model and find where the problem lies. Good luck.

Please holler if I can help.

Ensuring Your Selection of The Brass Ring (or Contact Me)

I've gone round and round with this whole book idea/concept. I've been up and down about self-publishing again, or looking for another option.

Obviously I optioned to self-publish. It's just way easier than trying to go without an agent or trying to find an agent, paying someone to be an agent, or whatever.

I lose a lot. I lose all the editing that comes along with setting out on your own. Of course when I read some of the books I read I wonder "and this was edited?" and often wonder that out loud.

I lose the publicity a big house I guess provides.

I lose all the marketing, distribution, advertising and other intangibles. Well, okay.

I decided to go it by myself. My book's out here now. It's formatted the way I want and printed how I choose.

Most importantly, I'm selling this thing at cost. Not writing, editing, formatting, publicizing cost, but just at what https://www.createspace.com/ says is the lowest cost I should sell it for, so I guess they make a little money and I get my work out there.

Why?

Why not seek profit.

My profit comes from all the smiling children and the lives that will be changed. My profit…

Not really.

My profit comes from my speaking engagements.

I have spoken once to a crowd of about 7,500. Most my audiences hover in the "hundreds" range and many are in the 20 and 30 range.

I've done keynotes and ending conferences. I've done all-day workshops and "lunch-and-learns."

I've extended this great adventure from north to south and east to west, coast-to-coast.

Exclusive of travel and lodging I am probably not the cheapest guy. My after action surveys though have always been stellar. That's not being a braggart; it's simply relaying what has been my history…to date.

☆☆☆☆☆ _____

☆☆☆☆☆ _____

☆☆☆☆☆ _____

☆☆☆☆☆ _____

☆☆☆☆☆ _____

☆☆☆☆☆ _____

☆☆☆☆☆ _____

So, for an hour, I'm in the $4,000 and up range ($1,500 for most not-for-profits) and plus expenses.

That preceding we can discuss, but that gives you an idea.

I've spoken extensively on just about everything related to human resources and personnel. From…well…duh…hiring through leadership challenges through management concerns through balancing families and stress. One of my primary areas of expertise is how to give great public presentations.

So my scope is broad and the expanse of my areas I feel comfortable with pretty broad as well. Interested?

My speaking, my profit, is why I sell this book at cost. So, I hope you'll have an interest, give me a shout, rcastle263@gmail.com.

Appendix
Your Table of Contents
Journaling Adventure
(open this from back of this book)

My Journal
My contents

www.ingramcontent.com/pod-product-compliance
Lightning Source LLC
Chambersburg PA
CBHW070227190526
45169CB00001B/103